1st EDITION

Perspectives on Diseases and Disorders

Alcoholism

Jacqueline Langwith

Book Editor

Detroit • New York • San Francisco • New Haven, Conn • Waterville, Maine • London

Christine Nasso, *Publisher*
Elizabeth Des Chenes, *Managing Editor*

For more information, contact:
Greenhaven Press
27500 Drake Rd.
Farmington Hills, MI 48331-3535
Or you can visit our Internet site at gale.cengage.com

Articles in Greenhaven Press anthologies are often edited for length to meet page requirements. In addition, original titles of these works are changed to clearly present the main thesis and to explicitly indicate the author's opinion. Every effort is made to ensure that Greenhaven Press accurately reflects the original intent of the authors. Every effort has been made to trace the owners of copyrighted material.

Cover image © 2009 Jupiterimages

LIBRARY OF CONGRESS CATALOGING-IN-PUBLICATION DATA

Alcoholism / Jacqueline Langwith, editor.
     p. cm. -- (Perspectives on diseases and disorders)
  Includes bibliographical references and index.
  ISBN 978-0-7377-4550-4 (hardcover)
  1. Alcoholism--Juvenile literature. 2. Drinking of alcoholic beverages--
Juvenile literature. I. Langwith, Jacqueline.
  HV5066.A395 2009
  616.86'1--dc22
                                                                    2009025869

Printed in the United States of America
1 2 3 4 5 6 7 13 12 11 10 09

CONTENTS

FOREWORD

"Medicine, to produce health, has to examine disease."
—Plutarch

Independent research on a health issue is often the first step to complement discussions with a physician. But locating accurate, well-organized, understandable medical information can be a challenge. A simple Internet search on terms such as "cancer" or "diabetes," for example, returns an intimidating number of results. Sifting through the results can be daunting, particularly when some of the information is inconsistent or even contradictory. The Greenhaven Press series Perspectives on Diseases and Disorders offers a solution to the often overwhelming nature of researching diseases and disorders.

From the clinical to the personal, titles in the Perspectives on Diseases and Disorders series provide students and other researchers with authoritative, accessible information in unique anthologies that include basic information about the disease or disorder, controversial aspects of diagnosis and treatment, and first-person accounts of those impacted by the disease. The result is a well-rounded combination of primary and secondary sources that, together, provide the reader with a better understanding of the disease or disorder.

Each volume in Perspectives on Diseases and Disorders explores a particular disease or disorder in detail. Material for each volume is carefully selected from a wide range of sources, including encyclopedias, journals, newspapers, nonfiction books, speeches, government documents, pamphlets, organization newsletters, and position papers. Articles in the first chapter provide an authoritative, up-to-date overview that covers symptoms, causes and effects, treatments, cures, and medical advances. The second chapter presents a substantial number of opposing viewpoints on controversial treatments and other current debates relating to the volume topic. The third chapter offers a variety of personal perspectives on the disease or disorder. Patients, doctors, caregivers, and loved ones represent just some of the voices found in this narrative chapter.

Each Perspectives on Diseases and Disorders volume also includes:

- An **annotated table of contents** that provides a brief summary of each article in the volume.
- An **introduction** specific to the volume topic.
- Full-color **charts and graphs** to illustrate key points, concepts, and theories.
- Full-color **photos** that show aspects of the disease or disorder and enhance textual material.
- **"Fast Facts"** that highlight pertinent additional statistics and surprising points.
- A **glossary** providing users with definitions of important terms.
- A **chronology** of important dates relating to the disease or disorder.
- An annotated list of **organizations to contact** for students and other readers seeking additional information.
- A **bibliography** of additional books and periodicals for further research.
- A detailed **subject index** that allows readers to quickly find the information they need.

Whether a student researching a disorder, a patient recently diagnosed with a disease, or an individual who simply wants to learn more about a particular disease or disorder, a reader who turns to Perspectives on Diseases and Disorders will find a wealth of information in each volume that offers not only basic information, but also vigorous debate from multiple perspectives.

INTRODUCTION

*T*eratology and *dysmorphology* are terms that are used to describe the study of congenital malformation. Disfiguring birth defects can result from genetic abnormalities, such as having too few or too many chromosomes. They can also result from fetal exposure to chemical or physical agents, bacteria or viruses, infections, and alcohol. In the 1970s David W. Smith, a researcher at the University of Washington Medical School, began recognizing a pattern of physical anomalies in infants born to mothers with a history of maternal alcohol consumption. Fetal alcohol syndrome (FAS) was first coined in the medical literature by Smith and his colleagues in an article published in the medical journal *Lancet.* Since then there has been much research on the connection between maternal drinking and birth defects. Despite a large amount of research attention, however, there is still a debate about exactly how much maternal alcohol consumption causes FAS. Some experts recommend that pregnant women abstain completely from alcohol, while others say light or moderate drinking is all right.

In a 1973 *Lancet* article, Smith and his associates presented the case histories of eight unrelated children born to mothers who were chronic alcoholics. All the children showed a similar pattern of craniofacial, limb, and cardiovascular defects associated with growth deficiencies and developmental delays while in the womb. The children's facial structures were distinctly abnormal, according to Smith. Their heads were small, and their jaws were underdeveloped and looked either small or protruding. They had flat faces, low nasal bridges, thin upper lips, drooping eyelids, and small eye openings. In addition to the facial effects, abnormalities related to the fingers or toes and some cardiac deficiencies were also noted. According to Smith and his colleagues, the similarity in the pattern of malformation noted among the eight children suggested that they had all been exposed to the same toxic agent in the womb. Based on the mothers' chronic alcoholism, they suggested ethanol (i.e., alcohol) as the most likely possibility.

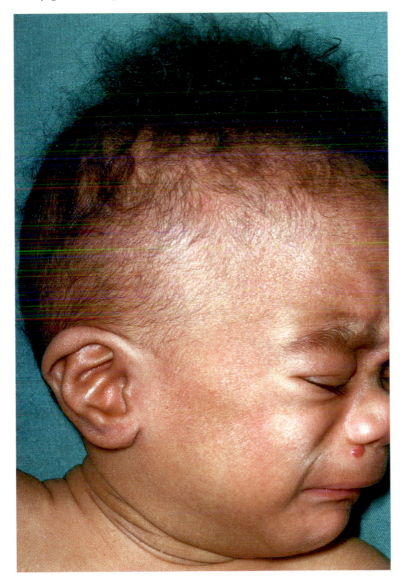

Research into fetal alcohol syndrome has revealed a connection between birth defects and a mother's drinking alcohol during pregnancy. (© Medical-on-Line/Alamy)

Over thirty years later, FAS is a well-characterized spectrum of diseases known to cause facial anomalies, growth deficiencies, and central nervous system dysfunction. The U.S. Institute of Medicine has identified five different disorders within the FAS spectrum, which are based on the presence of several different physical and physiological characteristics and whether or not maternal drinking is confirmed. The severity of the disorders within the spectrum vary based on many factors. Scientists suspect that the timing of drinking during the developmental cycle, the infant's genetics, and the mother's age, race, overall health status, and whether or not she smokes may all play a role in determining the severity of FAS.

According to the U.S. Centers for Disease Control and Prevention (CDC), the Mayo Clinic, and many other health organizations, FAS is 100 percent preventable, and women should completely abstain from alcohol while pregnant. The CDC says: "When a pregnant woman drinks alcohol, so does her unborn baby. There is no known safe amount of alcohol to drink while pregnant and there also does not appear to be a safe time to drink during pregnancy either. Therefore, it is recommended that women abstain from drinking alcohol at any time during pregnancy." The CDC also recommends that sexually active women who are not practicing birth control also abstain from drinking, because they could become pregnant and not know it for several weeks or more.

The March of Dimes says that FAS disorders can occur in babies whose mothers consume less than one drink a week. The March of Dimes points to a 2007 study that suggested that female children of women who drank less than one drink a week were more likely to have behavioral and emotional problems at four and eight years of age. The March of Dimes says other studies report behavioral and learning problems in children exposed to moderate

drinking during pregnancy, including attention and memory problems, hyperactivity, impulsivity, poor social and communication skills, psychiatric problems, and alcohol and drug use.

Despite the apparent facts that FAS is caused by alcohol consumption during pregnancy, there are many physicians who tell women it is all right to drink in moderation. These physicians believe FAS is caused by chronic and heavy alcohol consumption or binge drinking and that an occasional glass of wine during pregnancy is all right.

The March of Dimes says its research has found that FAS disorders can occur in babies whose mothers drink less than one drink per week. (© Graham Dunn/Alamy)

Ernest Abel and Robert Sokol of Wayne State University School of Medicine in Detroit are two of these physicians. According to Abel and Sokol:

> In the last two decades more than 5,000 articles have been published on the effects of alcohol during pregnancy. One might assume we'd now have some consensus about the dangers of occasional light drinking during pregnancy. Unfortunately, this isn't so. Our own sober (no pun intended) conclusion, based on a critical evaluation of the literature, is that there are no known clinically important risks to the fetus from an occasional drink during pregnancy.

Abel and Sokol offer some compelling evidence, albeit anecdotal, for their belief. First, the doctors say that about two-thirds of all Americans drink to some extent, and millions of mothers are included in this statistic. They also contend that historical evidence indicates the country's founding fathers and mothers drank far more than we do today. Abel and Sokol also say that women do not always tell the truth about how much drinking they do. According to the doctors: "Because of denial, actual alcohol intake is underreported by the abusive drinker—the individual most likely to be at risk for giving birth to a child with alcohol related birth defects. The risk to the fetus of what might appear to be '2 drinks a day' is undoubtedly the result of a much higher intake." Finally, Abel and Sokol argue that there have been no truly controlled experiments to tease out the real effects of fetal alcohol exposures. They say: "Alcohol is but one of many possible risk factors, such as social class, maternal illness, genetic susceptibility, smoking, diet, past health history, pregnancy complications, use of drugs and exposure to environmental pollutants." The doctors say these factors need to be accounted for in any study of FAS.

Abel and Sokol provide some thought-provoking arguments about occasional maternal drinking. However, the CDC, the March of Dimes, the U.S. surgeon general, and most health organizations are in consensus about the message they want women to hear, and that is that no amount of alcohol during pregnancy is safe.

The debate about maternal alcohol consumption is just one of many debates that surround alcoholism. In *Perspectives on Diseases and Disorders: Alcoholism,* the authors provide the latest statistics, diagnoses, treatments, and scientific discoveries about alcoholism. They also debate some contentious issues and provide personal perspectives on alcoholism.

CHAPTER 1

Understanding Alcoholism

An Overview of Alcohol-Induced Disorders

Bill Asenjo and Ken R. Wells

In the following article Bill Asenjo and Ken R. Wells discuss the symptoms, treatments, and diagnosis of alcoholism, a disease that has extensive health and social impacts. According to Asenjo and Wells, alcohol abuse can affect people's physical and mental health, their relationships, and their work. The long-term effects of chronic alcohol use on the body include sleep disturbances, stomach inflammation, a weakened immune system, and cardiovascular damage. The authors say that the most common treatment for alcoholism involves detoxification, when the person stops drinking, and rehabilitation, when the person learns to avoid ever taking another drink. Recovery from alcoholism is a lifelong process, say Asenjo and Wells. Asenjo and Wells are nationally published health and medical writers.

*A*lcoholism is the popular term for alcohol abuse and alcohol dependence. These disorders involve repeated life problems that can be directly attributed to the use of alcohol. Both disorders can have serious

SOURCE: Bill Asenjo and Ken R. Wells, *The Gale Encyclopedia of Medicine*, Detroit: Gale, 2007. Reproduced by permission of Gale, a part of Cengage Learning.

Photo on facing page. The social impact of alcoholism is extensive, and women, who may tend to internalize their symptoms, are often not screened or diagnosed. (© Jaubert Bernard/Alamy)

consequences, affecting an individual's health and personal life, as well as having an impact on society at large.

Far-Reaching Effects

The effects of alcoholism are far reaching. Alcohol affects every body system, causing a wide range of health problems. Problems include poor nutrition, memory disorders, difficulty with balance and walking, liver disease (including cirrhosis and hepatitis), high blood pressure, muscle weakness (including the heart), heart rhythm disturbances, anemia, clotting disorders, decreased immunity to infections, gastrointestinal inflammation and irritation, acute and chronic problems with the pancreas, low blood sugar, high blood fat content, interference with reproductive fertility, and weakened bones.

Symptoms of Co-alcohol Dependence

- Psychological distress manifested in symptoms such as anxiety, aggression, anorexia nervosa, bulimia, depression, insomnia, hyperactivity, and suicidal tendency
- Psychosomatic illness (ailments that have no biological basis and clear up after the co-alcoholism clears up)
- Family violence or neglect
- Alcoholism or other drug abuse

On a personal level, alcoholism results in marital and other relationship difficulties, depression, unemployment, child abuse, and general family dysfunction.

Alcoholism causes or contributes to a variety of severe social problems including homelessness, murder, suicide, injury, and violent crime. Alcohol is a contributing factor in at least 50% of all deaths from motor vehicle accidents. In fact, about 100,000 deaths occur each year due to the effects of alcohol, of which 50% are due to injuries of some sort. According to a special report prepared for the

Alcoholism contributes to or causes a variety of social problems that include homelessness and violent crime.
(© Jeff Smith/Alamy)

U.S. Congress by the National Institute on Alcohol Abuse and Alcoholism, the impact of alcohol on society, including violence, traffic accidents, lost work productivity, and premature death, costs our nation an estimated $185 billion annually. In addition, it is estimated that approximately one in four children (20 million children or 29% of children up to 17 years of age) is exposed at some time to familial alcohol abuse, alcohol dependence, or both. Furthermore, it has been estimated that approximately 18% of adults experience an episode of alcohol abuse or dependence at some time during their lives.

There are probably a number of factors that work together to cause a person to become an alcoholic. Recent genetic studies have demonstrated that close relatives of an alcoholic are four times more likely to become alcoholics themselves. Furthermore, this risk holds true even for children who were adopted away from their biological families at birth and raised in a non-alcoholic adoptive family, with no knowledge of their biological family's difficulties with alcohol. More research is being conducted to determine if genetic factors could account for differences in alcohol metabolism that may increase the risk of an individual becoming an alcoholic.

Short-Term Effects of Alcohol

The symptoms of alcoholism can be broken down into two major categories: symptoms of acute alcohol use and symptoms of long-term alcohol use.

Alcohol exerts a depressive effect on the brain. The blood-brain barrier does not prevent alcohol from entering the brain, so the brain alcohol level will quickly become equivalent to the blood alcohol level. Alcohol's depressive effects result in difficulty walking, poor balance, slurring of speech, and generally poor coordination (accounting in part for the increased likelihood of injury). The affected person also may have impairment of peripheral vision. At higher alcohol levels, a person's breathing and heart rates will be slowed, and vomiting may occur (with a high risk of the vomit being breathed into the lungs, resulting in severe problems, including the possibility of pneumonia). Still higher alcohol levels may result in coma and death.

Long-Term Effects of Chronic Alcohol Use

Long-term use of alcohol affects virtually every organ system of the body:

Nervous system. An estimated 30–40% of all men in their teens and twenties have experienced alcoholic blackout, which occurs when drinking a large quantity of alcohol results in the loss of memory of the time surrounding the episode of drinking. Alcohol is well-known to cause sleep disturbances, so that overall sleep quality is affected. Numbness and tingling may occur in the arms and legs.

Two syndromes, which can occur together or separately, are known as Wernicke's and Korsakoff's syndromes [neurological disorders]. Both are due to the low thiamine (a form of vitamin B complex) levels found in alcoholics. Wernicke's syndrome results in disordered eye movements, very poor balance and difficulty walking, while Korsakoff's syndrome severely affects one's memory, preventing new learning from taking place.

Gastrointestinal system. Alcohol causes loosening of the muscular ring that prevents the stomach's contents from re-entering the esophagus. Therefore, the acid from the stomach flows backward into the esophagus, burning those tissues, and causing pain and bleeding. Inflammation of the stomach also can result in bleeding and pain, and decreased desire to eat. A major cause of severe, uncontrollable bleeding (hemorrhage) in an alcoholic is the development of enlarged (dilated) blood vessels within the esophagus, which are called esophageal varices. These varices actually are developed in response to liver disease, and are extremely prone to bursting and hemorrhaging. Diarrhea is a common symptom, due to alcohol's effect on the pancreas. In addition, inflammation of the pancreas (pancreatitis) is a serious and painful problem in alcoholics. Throughout the intestinal tract, alcohol interferes with the absorption of nutrients, creating a malnourished state. Because alcohol is broken down (metabolized) within the liver, the organ is severely affected by constant levels of alcohol. Alcohol interferes with a number of important chemical processes that also occur in the liver. The liver begins to enlarge and fill with fat (fatty liver), fibrous scar tissue interferes with the liver's normal structure and function (cirrhosis), and the liver may become inflamed (hepatitis).

Blood. Alcohol can cause changes to all the types of blood cells. Red blood cells become abnormally large. White blood cells (important for fighting infections) decrease in number, resulting in a weakened immune system.

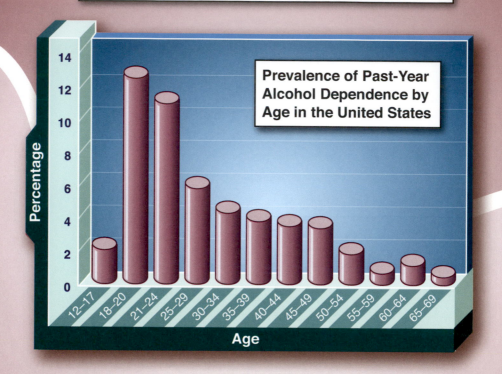

Young Adults Are Most at Risk for Alcohol Problems

Prevalence of Past-Year Alcohol Dependence by Age in the United States

Percentage (y-axis): 0, 2, 4, 6, 8, 10, 12, 14

Age (x-axis): 12–17, 18–20, 21–24, 25–29, 30–34, 35–39, 40–44, 45–49, 50–54, 55–59, 60–64, 65–69

Taken from: "Alcohol Research: A Lifespan Perspective," *Alcohol Alert*, National Institute on Alcohol Abuse and Alcoholism, January 2008. Source: NIAAA National Epidemiological Survey on Alcohol and Related Conditions (NESARC) data (18–60+ years of age) and Substance Abuse and Mental Health Administration (SAMHSA) 2003 National Survey on Drug Use and Health (NSDUH) (12–17 years of age).

This places alcoholics at increased risk for infections, and is thought to account in part for the increased risk of cancer faced by alcoholics (10 times the risk for nonalcoholics). Platelets and blood clotting factors are affected, causing an increased risk of bleeding.

Heart. Small amounts of alcohol cause a drop in blood pressure, but with increased use, alcohol begins to increase blood pressure into a dangerous range. High levels of fats circulating in the bloodstream increase the risk of heart disease. Heavy drinking results in an increase in heart size, weakening of the heart muscle, abnormal heart rhythms, a risk of blood clots forming within the chambers of the heart, and a greatly increased risk of stroke (due to a blood clot from the heart entering the circulatory system, going to the brain, and blocking a brain blood vessel).

Reproductive system. Heavy drinking has a negative effect on fertility in both men and women, by decreasing testicle and ovary size, and interfering with both sperm and egg production. When pregnancy is achieved in an alcoholic woman, the baby has a great risk of being born with fetal alcohol syndrome, which causes distinctive facial defects, lowered IQ, and behavioral problems.

Diagnosing Alcohol-Related Problems

Two different types of alcohol-related difficulties have been identified. The first is called *alcohol dependence,* which refers to a person who literally depends on the use of alcohol. Three of the following traits must be present to diagnose alcohol dependence:

- tolerance, meaning that a person becomes accustomed to a particular dose of alcohol, and must increase the dose in order to obtain the desired effect
- withdrawal, meaning that a person experiences unpleasant physical and psychological symptoms when he or she does not drink alcohol
- the tendency to drink more alcohol than one intends (once an alcoholic starts to drink, he or she finds it difficult to stop)
- being unable to avoid drinking or stop drinking once started
- having large blocks of time taken up by alcohol use
- choosing to drink at the expense of other important tasks or activities
- drinking despite evidence of negative effects on one's health, relationships, education, or job

Diagnosis is sometimes brought about when family members call an alcoholic's difficulties to the attention of a physician. A clinician may begin to be suspicious when a patient suffers repeated injuries or begins to experience medical problems related to the use of alcohol. In fact, some estimates suggest that about 20% of a physician's patients will be alcoholics.

Diagnosis is aided by administering specific psychological assessments that try to determine what aspects of a person's life may be affected by his or her use of alcohol. Determining the exact quantity of alcohol that a person drinks is of much less importance than determining how his or her drinking affects relationships, jobs, educational goals, and family life. In fact, because the metabolism (how the body breaks down and processes) of alcohol is so individual, the quantity of alcohol consumed is not part of the criteria list for diagnosing either alcohol dependence or alcohol abuse.

One simple tool for beginning the diagnosis of alcoholism is called the CAGE questionnaire. It consists of four questions, with the first letters of each key word spelling out the word CAGE:

- Have you ever tried to *Cut* down on your drinking?
- Have you ever been *Annoyed* by anyone's comments about your drinking?
- Have you ever felt *Guilty* about your drinking?
- Do you ever need an *Eye-opener* (a morning drink of alcohol) to start the day?

Other, longer lists of questions exist to help determine the severity and effects of a person's alcohol use. Given the recent research pointing to a genetic basis for alcoholism, it is important to ascertain whether anyone else in the person's family has ever suffered from alcoholism.

Detoxification—the First Step in Treatment

Treatment of alcoholism has two parts. The first step in the treatment of alcoholism, called detoxification, involves helping the person stop drinking and ridding his or her body of the harmful (toxic) effects of alcohol. Because the person's body has become accustomed to alcohol, the person will need to be supported through withdrawal. Withdrawal will be different for different patients, depending on the severity of the alcoholism, as measured by the quantity of alcohol ingested daily and the length of time the patient has been an alcoholic. Withdrawal symptoms can range from mild to life-threatening. Mild withdrawal symptoms include nausea, achiness, diarrhea, difficulty sleeping, sweatiness, anxiety, and trembling. This phase is usually over in about three to five days. More severe effects of withdrawal can include hallucinations (in which a patient sees, hears, or feels something that is not actually real), seizures, an unbearable craving for more alcohol, confusion, fever, fast heart rate, high blood pressure, and delirium (a fluctuating level of consciousness). Patients at highest risk for the most severe symptoms of withdrawal (referred to as delirium tremens) are those with other medical problems, including malnutrition, liver disease, or Wernicke's syndrome. Delirium tremens usually begin[s] about three to five days after the patient's last drink, progressing from the more mild symptoms to the more severe, and may last a number of days.

Patients going through only mild withdrawal are simply monitored carefully to make sure that more severe symptoms do not develop. No medications are necessary, however. Treatment of a patient suffering the more severe effects of withdrawal may require the use of sedative medications to relieve the discomfort of withdrawal and to avoid the potentially life-threatening complications of high blood pressure, fast heart rate, and seizures. Drugs called benzodiazapines are helpful in those patients suffering from hallucinations. Because of the patient's nausea, fluids may need to be given through a vein (intravenously), along with some necessary sugars and salts. It is crucial that thiamine be included in the fluids, because thiamine is usually quite low in alcoholic patients, and deficiency of thiamine is responsible for the Wernicke-Korsakoff syndrome.

Rehabilitation—the Next Step

After cessation of drinking has been accomplished, the next steps involve helping the patient avoid ever taking another drink. This phase of treatment is referred to as rehabilitation. The best programs incorporate the family into the therapy, because the family has undoubtedly been severely affected by the patient's drinking. Some therapists believe that family members, in an effort to deal with their loved one's drinking problem, sometimes develop patterns of behavior that accidentally support or "enable" the patient's drinking. This situation is referred to as "co-dependence," and must be addressed in order to successfully treat a person's alcoholism.

Sessions led by peers, where recovering alcoholics meet regularly and provide support for each other's recoveries, are considered among the best methods of preventing a return to drinking (relapse). Perhaps the most well-known such group is called Alcoholics Anonymous, which uses a "12-step" model to help people avoid drinking. These steps involve recognizing the destructive power that alcohol has held over the alcoholic's life, looking to a higher power for help in overcoming the problem, and reflecting on the ways in which the use of alcohol has hurt others and, if possible, making amends to those people. According to a recent study reported by the American Psychological Association (APA), anyone, regardless of his or her religious beliefs or lack of religious beliefs, can benefit from participation in 12-step programs such as Alcoholics Anonymous (AA) or Narcotics Anonymous (NA). The number of visits to 12-step self-help groups exceeds the number of visits to all mental health professionals combined.

Medications and Alternative Treatments

There are also medications that may help an alcoholic avoid returning to drinking. These have been used with variable success. Disulfiram (Antabuse) is a drug which, when mixed with alcohol, causes unpleasant reactions including nausea, vomiting, diarrhea, and trembling. Naltrexone, along with a similar compound, Nalmefene, can be helpful in limiting the effects of a relapse. Acamprosate is helpful in preventing relapse. None of these medications would be helpful unless the patient was also willing to work very hard to change his or her behavior. In 2004, a new compound was discovered that blocks actions of chemicals in the brain that may lead to relapses. Clinical tests were still underway as of mid-2007, but development of such a drug could have great potential in the medical management of alcoholism. Another study that year found that topiramate (Topamax), an anti-seizure medication, was effective in treating alcohol dependence in 150 participants in a clinical trial. The authors called for further study of this possible treatment.

Alternative treatments can be a helpful adjunct for the alcoholic patient, once the medical danger of withdrawal has passed. Because many alcoholics have very stressful lives (whether because of or leading to the alcoholism is sometimes a matter of debate), many of the treatments for alcoholism involve dealing with and relieving stress. These include massage, meditation, and hypnotherapy. The malnutrition of long-term alcohol use is addressed by nutrition-oriented practitioners with careful attention to a healthy diet and the use of nutritional supplements such as vitamins A, B complex, and C, as well as certain fatty acids, amino acids, zinc, magnesium, and selenium. Herbal treatments include milk thistle (*Silybum marianum*), which is thought to protect the liver against damage. Other herbs are thought to be helpful for the patient suffering

> **FAST FACT**
> Among the 17 million heavy drinkers aged twelve or older, 31.3 percent were also illicit drug users, according to the 2007 National Survey on Drug Use and Health.

through withdrawal. Some of these include lavender (*Lavandula officinalis*), skullcap (*Scutellaria lateriflora*), chamomile (*Matricaria recutita*), peppermint (*Mentha piperita*), yarrow (*Achillea millefolium*), and valerian (*Valeriana officinalis*). Acupuncture is believed to both decrease withdrawal symptoms and to help improve a patient's chances for continued recovery from alcoholism.

Recovery and Prevention

Recovery from alcoholism is a life-long process. In fact, people who have suffered from alcoholism are encouraged to refer to themselves ever after as "a recovering alcoholic," never a recovered alcoholic. This is because most researchers in the field believe that since the potential for alcoholism is still part of the individual's biological and psychological makeup, one can never fully recover from alcoholism. The potential for relapse (returning to illness) is always there, and must be acknowledged and respected. Statistics suggest that, among middle-class alcoholics in stable financial and family situations who have undergone treatment, 60% or more can be successful at an attempt to stop drinking for at least a year, and many for a lifetime.

Prevention must begin at a relatively young age since the first instance of intoxication (drunkenness) usually occurs during the teenage years. In fact, a 2004 study found that girls experimented with alcohol and cigarettes at a younger age—20% by seventh grade—than boys. It is particularly important that teenagers who are at high risk for alcoholism—those with a family history of alcoholism, an early or frequent use of alcohol, a tendency to drink to drunkenness, alcohol use that interferes with school work, a poor family environment, or a history of domestic violence—receive education about alcohol and its long-term effects. How this is best achieved, without irritating the youngsters and thus losing their attention, is the subject of continuing debate and study.

Unraveling the Genetics of Alcoholism

Patrick Perry, interview with John Nurnberger

In the following article Patrick Perry of the *Saturday Evening Post* interviews John Nurnberger, the director of the Institute of Psychiatric Research at Indiana University School of Medicine. Nurnberger discusses how families that are vulnerable to alcoholism are helping scientists understand the role of genetics in alcohol abuse. According to Nurnberger, scientists have linked specific genes and certain brain activity to alcoholism. Nurnberger says that understanding the genetic and biochemical mechanisms that make someone vulnerable to alcoholism can help scientists devise better treatments for alcohol addiction. Perry is managing editor at *The Saturday Evening Post*.

Historically, alcoholic behavior was blamed on a character flaw or weakness of will. After all, couldn't people stop drinking if they really wanted to? While the stigma surrounding alcoholism continues, scientists have

SOURCE: Patrick Perry, "Unraveling the Genetics of Alcoholism, an Interview with John Nurnberger," *Saturday Evening Post*, vol. 279, September/October 2007, pp. 50–54. © 2007 Saturday Evening Post Society. Reproduced by permission.

gained considerably more insight into how genes and environment interact to affect vulnerability to alcoholism—knowledge that is key to reducing the disease's exacting toll on individuals, families, and society.

As more genes are linked to the development of alcohol dependence and substance abuse, the findings will prove useful in developing tools for better gauging individual risk for the disease and identifying those with alcohol problems. Emerging genetic and environmental insights have also paved the way to the discovery of new therapies targeting specific genes or treatments tailored to individual backgrounds.

The [*Saturday Evening*] *Post* spoke with John Nurnberger, M.D., Ph.D., director of the Institute of Psychiatric Research at Indiana University School of Medicine and a leading researcher on the genetics of alcoholism for decades.

Using High-Risk Families to Unravel the Genetics of Alcoholism

Post: Could you tell us about your work with the Collaborative Study on the Genetics of Alcoholism (COGA), and how alcoholics and family members have helped?

Dr. Nurnberger: COGA is a study that has been continuously supported and funded by the National Institute on Alcohol Abuse and Alcoholism (NIAAA) starting in 1989. Drs. Henri Begleiter from the State University of New York and Ted Reich at Washington University in St. Louis helped launch and direct the initial study, which involved six sites around the country: University of California San Diego, University of Iowa, University of Connecticut, SUNY Downstate Medical Center in Brooklyn, Washington University in St. Louis, and Indiana University in Indianapolis.

For the past 18 years [since 1989], we have collaborated to identify families through persons diagnosed with

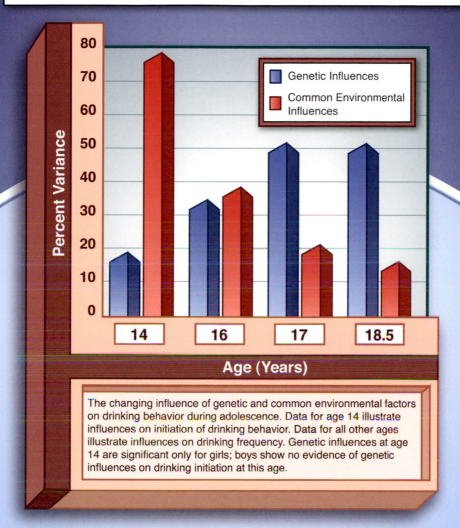

Genetic Factors in Drinking Behavior Become More Important as Adolescents Get Older

Percent Variance

- Genetic Influences
- Common Environmental Influences

Age (Years)

14 16 17 18.5

The changing influence of genetic and common environmental factors on drinking behavior during adolescence. Data for age 14 illustrate influences on initiation of drinking behavior. Data for all other ages illustrate influences on drinking frequency. Genetic influences at age 14 are significant only for girls; boys show no evidence of genetic influences on drinking initiation at this age.

Taken from: Richard Rose and Danielle Dick, "Gene-Environment Interplay in Adolescent Drinking Behavior," National Institute on Alcohol Abuse and Alcoholism, 2001.

alcohol dependence located at treatment facilities. Once we identified the individual, we would obtain permission to contact relatives of the person to discuss diagnoses in the extended family. We would then perform a brain wave study and take blood for DNA analysis.

In this way COGA established a huge database of information on 12,000 persons across the country. We organized the information to illuminate conditions that surfaced in families with a vulnerability to alcohol dependence and also to uncover the relationship of the brain electrical activity and DNA markers to those conditions.

Our group published a number of reports on findings from this sample over the years. We found that a variety of conditions go along with alcohol dependence in families, including dependence on various drugs—marijuana, opiates, tobacco, stimulants, and sedatives. We also noted that a constellation of anxiety and depressive disorders tend to cluster with alcohol problems.

In addition, we observed particular electrical activity signatures in the brain and specific single genes, such as those coding for GABRA2 (a receptor for a transmitter chemical that inhibits other signals), ADH4 (which breaks down alcohol in the body), and CHRM2 (another brain transmitter receptor).

COGA remains very active in various ways: one, we're looking for additional genes in the families we have been studying; and two, we identified adolescents in these families and are following them over time. This is a special high-risk population, and we're trying to determine risk and protective factors that impact young people growing up in families with multiple alcohol-dependent relatives. We are now at a point where some young people in the group are experiencing problems with alcohol but others are not, providing insights into how genes interact with family experience.

In doing the adolescent study, one interesting finding is that the pattern related to specific genes is unexpected. For example, in young people with genetic variations in the GABRA2 neurotransmitter receptor gene, we expected to see alcohol problems and we didn't. Instead, we observed conduct disorder. While you have to study adults to see the alcohol problem, in kids it's more behavior problems. When you look at persons who have the ADH4 gene variant, they begin drinking very early. When you observe persons with the CHRM2 gene variant, they experience depression and anxiety at greater rates as children. Later, they may develop alcohol problems.

Treatment Insights Have Emerged

What other insights have emerged?

A number of developments parallel the work we are doing. Some involve the identification of specific medications that reduce the risk of alcohol dependence, including naltrexone and acamprosate, which are used to reduce craving and risk of relapse.

Are 12-step programs like Alcoholics Anonymous still cornerstones of treatment?

Over the years Alcoholics Anonymous has been the most successful single treatment available for alcohol dependence. It still is. The A.A. Twelve Step Program has been adapted for many situations. For example, when adolescents and people with dual diagnoses, such as depression or anxiety, need help with substance abuse problems, A.A. is used. A series of psychotherapies are also under investigation—for example, motivational enhancement.

Alcohol treatment is actually much more successful than people realize. People tend to get a negative picture regarding addiction and the prognosis for people with addiction. It's unwarranted, because many treatments are successful both short- and long-term. People with an effective course of treatment tend to do well for about a year or so initially. A number will then slip back into problems with alcohol, but they seek treatment again, and eventually those who keep trying will be able to maintain their sobriety. Alcoholism has to be thought of as a chronic condition that requires long-term treatment. With that attitude and

The Alcoholics Anonymous 12-step program has been the single most successful program for alcohol dependence. (Hank Morgan/Photo Researchers, Inc.)

the ability to support long-term monitoring and treatment, people can recover very successfully from these disorders.

Can someone with a vulnerability to alcoholism also inherit a predisposition to bipolar disorder, depression, or another disorder?

Yes. They both need to be treated. That's been one of the difficulties in the past. In someone with depression and alcohol dependence, if you just treat the depression without the alcohol problem, it won't be effective and vice versa; if you just treat the alcohol problem without thinking about the depression, that's likely also not to be effective. There is an increased risk of alcohol dependence in persons with bipolar illness or depression. About half of people with major depression or bipolar illness will experience problems with alcohol dependence or substance abuse. The risk is about three times over the general population.

Are we at a point where we tailor treatment to best address an individual's specific genetic profile?

Not yet. There are not too many instances in which a genetic test would be of particular value as part of an individual's medical exam for alcohol dependence. But things may change rapidly in the next few years.

Understanding What It Means to Be Vulnerable to Alcoholism

In your recent article in Scientific American, *you wrote, "Genetics is never destiny." What can physicians and members of high-risk families do with the emerging information about vulnerability to alcoholism or substance abuse?*

We are trying to understand the biochemical pathways to vulnerability so that new treatments can be designed. Just because a condition is related to genetics doesn't mean it can't be treated or altered. Genetic vulnerabilities are simply that—vulnerabilities. While you can't alter the DNA code you're born with, you can alter the way the genes are expressed and how your body makes proteins from that DNA. In fact, medications can change gene expression, as can exercise. In effect, you can help turn off or turn on various genes by what you do, what medications you take, and the foods that you eat. It's very important for people to realize that, because there is a prominent notion that "you've got a gene for this or that, therefore the condition is inevitable." That's not at all the case.

We have to think differently about how genes actually work. In the body, gene expression is a very malleable process. We are trying to understand what the specific genes are that relate to alcohol dependence and how they work. We know some of them already, such as the GABRA2, the ADH4, and the CHRM2 that I mentioned.

Will your research findings apply to other addictions, such as smoking?

Yes. There is a genetic profile for tobacco dependence, as well as for alcohol dependence. The two conditions overlap quite a bit. Some of the overlap relates to a general predilection to addiction, and some has to do with specific aspects of nicotine or alcohol. We're beginning to understand the interaction. New evidence regarding the treatment response for people with tobacco dependence is very interesting with regard to the ability of genetic tests to predict treatment response to bupropion (Wellbutrin), one of the agents used to help people stop smoking. It may be that bupropion treatment is very good for persons with certain gene variants, while another treatment modality will help persons with other gene variants.

In the course of meeting these families, has increased self-awareness of genetic risk helped individuals make more informed choices?

In our clinic, the information has helped persons with bipolar illness; that's where I have the greatest exposure to individuals over time. The knowledge makes a difference in the way people think about themselves and their vulnerabilities. If they know that they are vulnerable to a certain substance, they may not stay away from it initially. Over time and with experience, they learn. . . .

The Role of Genetics in Alcoholism

Are we overcoming the stigma associated with these disorders?

Psychiatric illness has been stigmatized. Some think it shameful that people with any disorder might have to see a psychiatrist. There's no reason to think this. The brain is an organ just like the heart. Things go wrong with the brain based on genetics, just like they might go wrong in the heart or liver based on genetics. As we understand more about the treatments people need, the stigma associated with who they are because of genetic vulnerability to anxiety, depression, or addiction will decrease. People will see that no matter what gene variant they were born with (and we all have some), they can do—or not do—things to make life better.

What percentage of vulnerability to alcohol dependence is related to genetics?

For alcohol dependence, about 50 percent is related to genetic factors and the other half to environmental factors, such as availability of alcohol and cultural factors. In comparison, the heritability of bipolar illness is about 80 percent, while the heritability of major depression is about 60 percent. Alcohol dependence is less heritable, but still substantially influenced by genetics. In general, there is rarely a situation where there's a 100 percent chance that someone is going to inherit the disorder, except in a single-gene condition, such as Huntington's disease. Most of the diseases we study and treat are conditions of complex inheritance, where there is an increased or a decreased risk.

Could you discuss the connection between variations in basic physiology and individual susceptibility to alcohol problems?

There is actually a protective effect in many persons from East Asian populations who have variant forms of the enzyme aldehyde dehydrogenase (ALDH2). These persons tend to build up acetaldehyde—a byproduct of the metabolism of alcohol—which causes them to have low tolerance for alcohol. After one or two drinks, they may get a flushed feeling, feel uncomfortable,

FAST FACT

Studies indicate that 60 to 75 percent of people in alcohol treatment programs smoke cigarettes, and 40 to 50 percent are heavy smokers, consuming more than a pack a day.

develop a rapid pulse, experience nausea or reddening of the skin. Persons with this variant have a much lower risk of developing alcohol dependency because they just don't tolerate the alcohol very long. We don't see this in the general U.S. population, but we do see more subtle effects related to variants of the alcohol dehydrogenase (ADH) enzyme, and some of these variants appear protective as well—a finding that emerged in the last few years.

Diagnosing Alcohol Disorders

What is the clinical difference between alcohol dependence and alcohol abuse?

Alcohol dependence is a more severe condition. We diagnose alcohol abuse if a person has one persistent symptom—driving while intoxicated or using alcohol in a way that it interferes with work or gets a person in trouble socially. If the symptom persists over time, that would be enough for a diagnosis of alcohol abuse.

Alcohol dependence, on the other hand, is a more pervasive characteristic. The diagnosis requires three or more symptoms that include loss of control, tolerance and withdrawal, giving up important activities in order to drink, and persistent drinking despite medical consequences. If the problems occur together over the course of a year or longer, we would call that alcohol dependence.

Are brain electrical activity patterns different between alcoholics and nonalcoholics? If so, could we include an EEG as a useful clinical tool in the diagnosis of alcoholism?

We use the electrical activity of the brain to provide information for research purposes, but not really for clinical purposes. Brain imaging could at some point be used for clinical purposes. But we are primarily trying to understand whether there is a difference in the electrical activity of the brain in persons vulnerable to alcohol dependence. We studied persons with alcohol problems and their relatives—those who drank and those who didn't.

We found consistent differences in attention, response to stimuli like sounds and lights, and the predominant frequency of brain wave activity. It appears that persons vulnerable to alcohol dependence have measurable brain differences in terms of the electrical activity. For one, there appeared to be decreased attention to important stimuli in persons vulnerable to alcohol dependence. It also appeared as though there was decreased evidence of inhibition in the cortex area of the brain, which could be related to increased impulsivity. We believe it relates to the activity of GABA, a major inhibitory neurotransmitter in the brain. Like many of our findings, the hope is that these observations may one day translate into a target for intervention.

In studies of children of alcoholics who were adopted by nondrinking families, does alcohol tend to emerge less often, harking back to the role of the environment?

While we haven't done adoption studies in Indiana, studies have been done, primarily in Scandinavian countries that have central records of adoption and psychiatric hospitalization that investigators can access. It does appear that the chance for alcohol dependence is greater in adopted-away children of alcoholics, even if they are not brought up in families with the alcoholic person. One still faces increased risk from the genes.

A Researcher's Hope

What is your overall hope by identifying genetic influences on vulnerability?

Identifying genetic influences helps us on the road to self-knowledge and leads to strategies for optimal health and a productive life. The field is opening up in front of us. We will witness very real changes in the next couple of decades.

The Five Different Types of Alcoholics in the United States

Joan Arehart-Treichel

In the following article Joan Arehart-Treichel discusses the significance of knowing that there are five different subtypes of alcoholics in the United States. According to Arehart-Treichel, researchers applied statistical methods to data containing information about people seeking or obtaining treatment for alcohol abuse, as well as people who are considered to have an alcohol problem but have not sought treatment. The data revealed five different groups, or subtypes, of alcoholics in the United States. The researchers were surprised to find that young adults make up the biggest group of alcohol abusers. Arehart-Treichel is a health and medicine author.

A study in press with *Drug and Alcohol Dependence* provides what may be the clearest picture yet of Americans with alcohol dependence.

The study analyzed the clinical features of 1,484 Americans found to be alcohol-dependent through the 2001–

2002 National Epidemiological Survey on Alcohol and Related Conditions and then grouped those persons according to their clinical features.

No "Typical" Alcoholic

The study found that there is no such thing as a "typical alcoholic," rather that alcohol-dependent subjects tend to fall into five subtypes—young adult, young antisocial, intermediate familial, functional, and chronic severe.

- *Young adult subtype.* This is the most common alcohol-dependent subtype, constituting 32 percent of alcohol-dependent Americans. They are typically young, male adult drinkers with relatively low rates of co-occurring substance abuse and other mental disorders. They have a 22 percent rate of familial alcoholism and rarely seek help for their drinking.
- *Young antisocial subtype.* This is the second most common category of alcohol-dependent individuals, constituting 21 percent of alcohol-dependent Americans. They are apt to be in their mid-20s and to have started drinking early. About half come from families with alcoholism, and about half have a diagnosis of antisocial personality disorder. Three-fourths of these individuals smoke cigarettes; two-thirds meet criteria for marijuana abuse or dependence. About a fourth use cocaine, and about a fifth abuse opioids. About one-third seek treatment for their drinking problem.
- *Intermediate familial subtype.* Nineteen percent of alcohol-dependent Americans fall into this category. They tend to be middle-aged, with about half coming from families in which a member has alcoholism. Almost half have experienced a major depression, and almost a quarter have been diagnosed with bipolar disorder. About one-fifth abuse marijuana or cocaine. One quarter of these people seek treatment for their drinking problem.

One of the five types of alcoholics is the antisocial type who is generally in his or her twenties and started drinking as a very young teen. (© Leila Cutler/Alamy)

- *Functional subtype.* Nineteen percent of alcohol-dependent Americans fall into this category. They are, on average, older than other subtype members and tend to drink in an excessive, although less severe, manner than other subtypes. They have the highest family income, are college-educated, and are most likely to be married. They also include the highest proportion of retired individuals. From a psychosocial perspective, they represent the highest functioning subtype of alcohol- dependent persons. Nonetheless, they may still ultimately be at significant risk of the biomedical consequences of alcohol dependence. Seventeen percent seek treatment for their drinking problem.
- *Chronic severe subtype.* This is the smallest category of alcohol-dependent Americans, constituting 9 percent of them. The subtype is composed mostly of middle-aged persons who had early onset of drinking. Over three-fourths come from families afflicted with alcoholism. This subtype has the highest probability of all the subtypes of having both first- and second-degree family members with alcohol dependence. Almost half have antisocial personality disorder. Of all the subtypes, they have the highest rate of major depression, social phobia, and bipolar, anxiety, and panic disorders. Over three-fourths smoke cigarettes. They often abuse substances in addition to alcohol. Two-thirds seek help for their drinking. They are the largest subgroup who seek treatment.

Surprised by the Number of Young Adults with Alcohol Problems

In an interview with *Psychiatric News*, lead researcher Howard Moss, M.D., associate director for clinical and translational research at the National Institute on Alcohol Abuse and Alcoholism, said the study's findings were unexpected.

Prevalence of the Five Subtypes of Alcohol Dependence in the United States

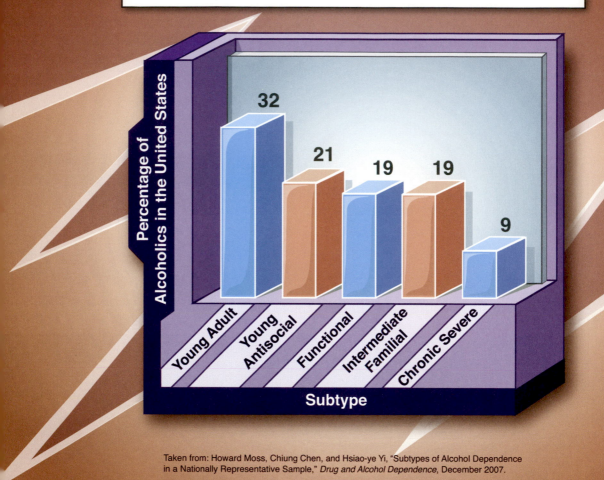

Taken from: Howard Moss, Chiung Chen, and Hsiao-ye Yi, "Subtypes of Alcohol Dependence in a Nationally Representative Sample," *Drug and Alcohol Dependence*, December 2007.

"We were surprised that so many of the individuals who met diagnostic criteria for alcohol dependence were young adults. We thought we were going to see a substantial proportion of folks with alcohol dependence being of the chronic recurring subtype that is seen in Veterans Administration hospitals and in other kinds of settings where people treat chronic disease. Another surprise was the breakout in terms of family history of alcohol problems and the fact that only about half the sample had familial transmission of alcohol dependence."

The study results suggest that certain therapies might work better with certain subtypes than with others, Moss said. In fact, he and his coworkers will now be attempting to see whether certain types of therapies work best for this or that subtype. Until such results are obtained, how should individuals in the various categories be treated?

Treatment Choices Vary for Each Subtype

"The young adult variety may be addressed with screening and brief intervention techniques rather than much more expensive approaches to therapeutic intervention," Moss advised. "It may also be—and again this is speculation, as we have to do the studies—that certain types of pharmacotherapies that are now available could be better targeted to this subgroup. For example, this subgroup might benefit from pharmacotherapy that reduces the reinforcing effect of alcohol."

Since the antisocial group has the worst prognosis of any of the subtypes, Moss said, "the focus there has to be on complete abstinence and elimination of other forms of substance abuse and also mainstreaming their behaviors so that they are much more like the rest of society."

"The functional subtype," Moss emphasized, "represents individuals who essentially have fewer psychosocial consequences from their alcohol dependence. So the focus of the therapy there needs to be on recognition of the impairment that their alcohol dependence is producing in their life and also focusing on either abstinence or a return to a much less hazardous level of drinking."

As for individuals with chronic severe alcohol dependence, "We would certainly assume that they are going

> **FAST FACT**
>
> A 2006 study in the *Archives of Pediatrics & Adolescent Medicine* found that 47 percent of alcoholics of any age had already met the diagnostic criteria for alcohol dependence by age twenty-one.

to need substantial treatment," said Moss. "They might benefit from therapies that are directed toward relapse prevention." Furthermore, this group is going to have substantial psychiatric comorbidity, he pointed out, "so we have to simultaneously address their alcohol use disorder as well as manage their psychopathology."

Charles O'Brien, M.D., Ph.D., a professor of psychiatry at the University of Pennsylvania, who was unaffiliated with the study, told *Psychiatric News* that this study marks an important step in subcategorizing alcoholism because it includes a community sample rather than simply examining the 25 percent who present for treatment; it is based on a large dataset, and the five subtypes seem quite recognizable based on the data used: family history, age of onset, and presence of other psychiatric disorders.

"The next step," he said, "[is to identify] biomarkers for even more precise subcategories, such as genotype or biochemical test."

Treating Alcoholism with Medication

Catherine Arnst

In the following article Catherine Arnst asserts that there is a growing body of evidence to support the theory that alcoholism is a true medical disease and not just a social ill. According to Arnst, alcoholism has long been treated as a behavioral issue and treated with Alcoholics Anonymous or other 12-step programs. However, recent attention by researchers and drug makers have led to the development of several new drugs that have helped some alcoholics resist their alcoholic cravings. Arnst says that the new antialcoholism drugs target the brain's addiction pathways. For instance, one drug reduces levels of the neurotransmitter glutamate, and this helps alcoholics who have quit drinking avoid relapse. She asserts that alcohol addiction medications may be able to help many alcoholics finally quit drinking for good. Arnst is a senior writer for *Business Week*, covering medicine and science issues.

SOURCE: Catherine Arnst, "Can Alcoholism Be Treated?" *Business Week*, April 11, 2005. Copyright © 2005 by McGraw-Hill, Inc. Reproduced by permission.

Dr. Olivier Ameisen is a 51-year-old cardiologist in Paris. He is also an alcoholic. Between 1997 and 2004, Ameisen was hospitalized numerous times for drinking. He went through years of rehabilitation programs and attended two Alcoholics Anonymous meetings a day, some 700 a year, for seven years. All to no avail. His craving for drink always overwhelmed his desire to quit.

By January, 2004, Ameisen came to believe his only hope would be a drug that could dampen those cravings. But despite the fact that alcoholism is widely recognized as a medical condition, there were only two medications available, and neither had worked for him. Ameisen researched the literature and came across rat studies showing that baclofen, a generic drug used to control muscle spasms, could suppress the desire to consume alcohol by interfering with the reward circuitry in the brain. It is also used to treat anxiety disorders, which afflict large numbers of alcoholics, including Ameisen.

The doctor decided to self-prescribe the drug at high doses. And he took the unusual step of writing himself up as a case study this past December in the journal *Alcohol & Alcoholism*. After nine months on baclofen, he reported that he had not had a drink since Jan. 9, 2004, and, more important, that he had experienced "no craving or desire for alcohol for the first time in my alcoholic life. Even in a restaurant with friends, I was indifferent to people drinking. This had never occurred before."

Ameisen's detailed report adds to a growing body of evidence that alcoholism—and addiction itself—has unique pathologic traits that can be corrected through chemical intervention. Drug researchers are now striving to bring science to bear on what was long treated as a social problem rather than a medical one. Over the last decade, sophisticated brain-imaging technologies have demonstrated that constant use of alcohol significantly alters the structure of the brain in ways that can last for months and even years, creating a chronic brain disease. With this knowledge in hand, the search is on for drugs that can restore the brain to its pre-drinking state.

Forest Laboratories Inc. started marketing one promising medicine in the U.S. in January. Campral, the first alcoholism drug to win Food & Drug Administration approval in 10 years, is designed to suppress alcohol cravings by targeting specific brain chemicals thrown out of balance by drinking. Alkermes Inc. filed for FDA approval of its own anti-craving drug, Vivitrex, on Apr. 1.

Converging Forces

Neither drug is new. Campral has been on the market in Europe for 15 years, and Vivitrex is a once-a-month, injectable form of naltrexone, a daily pill approved for alcoholism in 1994. Nor are Campral and Vivitrex miracle cures. Dr. Ameisen tried both, to no effect. Clinical trials have shown that they can help patients remain abstinent two to three times longer than those on placebo, but the relapse rate is high.

Still, these medicines prove the principle: Drugs that target the brain's addiction pathways can curb drinking. Scientists have also discovered that almost any addiction, be it alcohol, cocaine, nicotine, even gambling, involves many of the same pathways. A drug that treats one addiction may be effective against others. As a result, research in this field is rapidly accelerating. "I've been treating addiction for over 20 years, and for the first time I believe there is a convergence of various forces that will get medications out there," says Dr. Richard N. Rosenthal, chairman of the Psychiatry Dept. at St. Luke's-Roosevelt Hospital Center in New York. "The pharmaceutical industry is finally getting interested."

Drug companies have good reason to be paying attention—alcoholism is one of medicine's largest unmet

> **FAST FACT**
>
> Up to 80 percent of alcoholics suffer from thiamine deficiency, and some of them go on to develop Wernicke-Korsakoff syndrome, a serious brain disease.

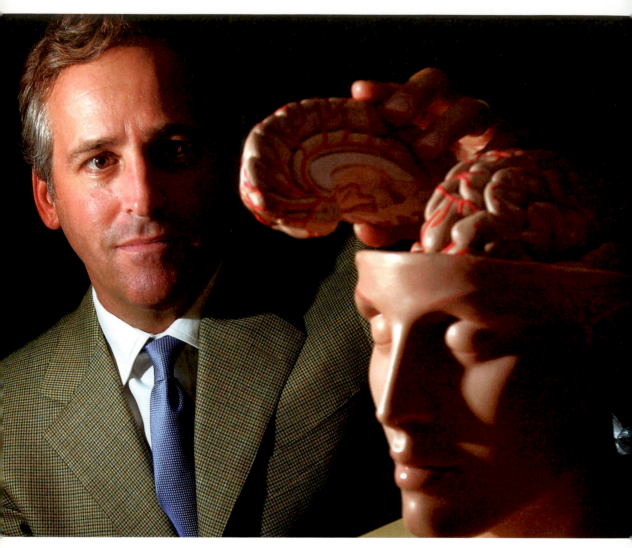

Richard Pops, chief executive officer of Alkermes, Inc., uses a brain model to illustrate the effects of his company's new alcohol treatment medication, Vivitrex. (AP Images)

needs. The National Institute on Alcohol Abuse and Alcoholism estimates that almost 18 million people in the U.S. abuse or are addicted to alcohol. They cost the nation some $185 billion a year in medical services, lost wages, and law enforcement resources. Yet each year only two million alcohol-dependent people seek treatment, and up to 90% relapse within four years.

Despite the huge number of sufferers, alcoholism was "underscienced" for years, says Alkermes CEO Richard F.

Pops. Since 1935, when Alcoholics Anonymous was founded, the vast majority of treatment efforts in the U.S. were based on AA's 12-step program, requiring behavioral changes and faith in a higher power. "The history of treatment in this country was not consistent with the idea that medicines could help," says Dr. Klye M. Kampman, associate professor of psychiatry at the University of Pennsylvania. "We were very moralistic."

For decades the only alcoholism drug in the U.S. was Antabuse, which causes people to vomit when they drink. Even now, only some 140,000 alcoholics in the U.S. receive medication for their disease, ranging from Antabuse to anti-depressants to anti-seizure drugs. There was no move to introduce Campral in the U.S. until Forest licensed it from Germany's Merck in 2001.

A clearer understanding of the biological underpinnings of alcoholism is opening the way to better drugs. Scientists have identified a number of genes that confer a predisposition to alcohol addiction. They have also found that the brain goes through profound changes when a person starts drinking to excess.

Alcohol releases a neurotransmitter called GABA (gamma-aminobutyric acid), instrumental in creating a sense of euphoria. Too much GABA can impair muscle control and slow reaction times, so the brain releases a stimulating chemical called glutamate to keep it in check. When alcohol is cut off, glutamate levels remain high and can cause irritability and discomfort. To relieve those feelings, the brain craves another drink. As more GABA and glutamate are released, brain cells change their structure to accommodate the excess chemicals, making them dependent on these levels. When alcohol is withdrawn, painful emotional and physical reactions are set off.

GABA may be the reason people drink, but glutamate is the reason they can't stop. This powerful neurotransmitter is a key player in the brain's learning centers, and excess amounts create deeply embedded memories of drinking. Years after a person quits, these memories can be triggered by a place, person, or even smell associated with drinking, setting off intense cravings. Such cue-induced cravings are the main reason for relapse. "They're why it can be easy to get off a drug, but it's very hard to stay off," says Dr. Herbert D. Kleber, director of the division on substance abuse at Columbia University.

Campral helps alcoholics resist these cravings by checking production of glutamate, bringing the brain's chemistry back into balance. Clinical studies of Campral have shown that after six months of treatment, 36% of patients were still abstinent, compared with 23.4% on placebo. Vivitrex dampens cravings by a slightly different mechanism, calming opioid receptors in the neurons that are overstimulated by alcohol. A recent study showed that Vivitrex can help people cut way down on alcohol bingeing. That's not the same as abstinence, but Dr. James C. Garbutt, an alcoholism researcher at the University of North Carolina at Chapel Hill, says reduced drinking is still meaningful in a disease that is remarkably resistant to treatment. "If you significantly reduce the number of heavy drinking days, you've made a big impact." Treatment specialists believe that Campral and Vivitrex may be most effective when used in combination.

Indifference at Last

Existing drugs approved for other purposes may end up being part of that combination. The field got a jolt last August from a study in *The Lancet* that showed that Topamax, an anti-seizure medicine from Johnson & Johnson, helped 13 of 55 patients abstain from drinking for a month. Dr. Bankole A. Johnson of the University of Texas Health Science Center at San Antonio, who headed the study, said the patients all started on the drug while still drinking, a significant breakthrough. Campral is taken after the patient quits.

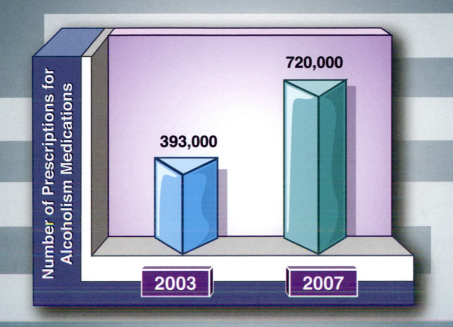

Taken from: Mark Tami et al. "Alcohol and Opioid Dependence Medications: Prescription Trends, Overall and by Physician Specialty," *Drug and Alcohol Dependence*, January 2009.

Still, no drug is recommended in a vacuum. "We are developing better and better medications, but they need to be taken in a therapeutic context," says Kleber—which may include AA and other types of behavioral therapies. Dr. Ameisen, for one, found it much easier to use the techniques he learned at AA while on baclofen. But it was the drug that changed his life. "At the end of my ninth month of complete liberation from symptoms of alcohol dependence, I remain indifferent to alcohol," he writes. "Abstinence has become natural to me."

The Global Burden of Harmful Use of Alcohol and Strategies to Reduce It

World Health Organization

In the following article the World Health Organization (WHO) maintains that harmful use of alcohol is a global public health concern. The WHO says that alcohol abuse causes neuropsychiatric disorders, liver disease, cardiovascular disease, cancers, infectious diseases, traffic deaths, and suicides. According to WHO, alcohol problems are a major concern in third world countries and in developed countries. The organization provides many strategies that countries, states, and communities can use to reduce alcohol consumption. A specialized agency of the United Nations, WHO acts as a coordinating authority on international public health.

Harmful use of alcohol is one of the main factors contributing to premature deaths and avoidable disease burden worldwide and has a major impact on public health. Although there are regional, national and local differences in levels, patterns and context

SOURCE: "Strategies to Reduce the Harmful Use of Alcohol: Report by the Secretariat," World Health Organization, 61st World Health Assembly, March 20, 2008. Reproduced by permission.

of drinking, in 2002 the harmful use of alcohol was estimated to cause about 2.3 million premature deaths worldwide (3.7% of global mortality) and to be responsible for
4.4% of the global burden of disease, even when protective
effects of low and moderate alcohol consumption on morbidity and mortality have been taken into consideration.

Harmful Use of Alcohol Causes Death and Disease

Harmful use of alcohol encompasses several aspects of
drinking. One is the volume drunk over time. The
strongest drinking-related predictor of many chronic illnesses is the cumulated amount of alcohol consumed over
a period of years. Other factors include the pattern of
drinking, in particular occasional or regular drinking to
intoxication; the drinking context, which may increase the
risks of intentional and unintentional injuries and of

According to the World
Health Organization,
an emerging concern
in third world countries
is the number of
traffic deaths that
result from alcohol-
related accidents.
(© Flirt/SuperStock)

transmission of certain infectious diseases; and the quality of the alcoholic beverage or its contamination with toxic substances such as methanol.

Harmful drinking is a major avoidable risk factor for neuropsychiatric disorders and other noncommunicable diseases such as cardiovascular diseases, cirrhosis of the liver and various cancers. For some diseases, such as breast cancer, there is no evidence of a threshold effect in the relationship between the risk and level of alcohol consumption. A significant proportion of the disease burden attributable to harmful drinking is determined by unintentional and intentional injuries, including those due to road traffic crashes, and suicides. Fatal alcohol-attributable injuries tend to occur in relatively young people. Some vulnerable or at-risk groups and individuals have increased susceptibility to the toxic, psychoactive and dependence-producing properties of alcohol.

Public health problems caused by harmful use of alcohol are considerable in countries with different levels of development and effectiveness of health systems. Globally, among 20 selected risk factors to health, harmful use of alcohol is the leading cause of death and disability in developing countries with low mortality, the third among the leading risk factors in developed countries, after tobacco and blood pressure, and eleventh in developing countries with high mortality rates. Awareness is growing of the impact of harmful use of alcohol on the burden of infectious diseases, including sexually-transmitted infections and HIV infection, through association with unsafe sexual behaviour and interference with effective treatment regimens and procedures.

Harmful Drinking Has Numerous Societal Impacts

Harmful drinking among young people and women is an increasing concern across many countries. Drinking to intoxication and heavy episodic drinking are frequent among adolescents and young adults, and the negative impact of alcohol use is greater in younger age groups of both sexes. The range of prenatal damage includes fetal alcohol syndrome and various physical defects and neurobiological deficits that impair development and social functioning. Harmful drinking affects not only those who drink, but also others and has consequences for society. There is growing evidence on alcohol's contribution to acute injuries associated with violence and traffic crashes involving pedestrians. The public health impact of alcohol-related road crashes could become even more marked

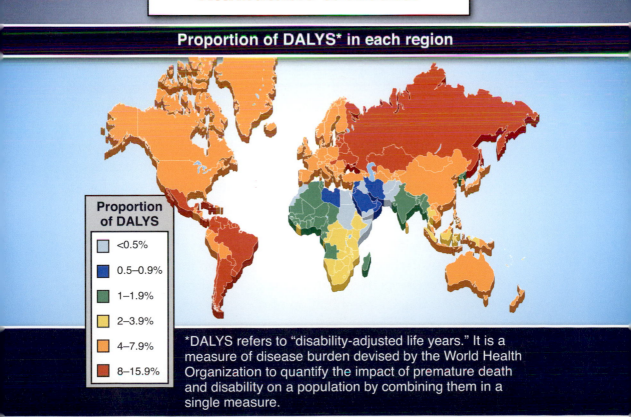

Worldwide Burden of Disease Attributable to Alcohol

Proportion of DALYS* in each region

Proportion of DALYS

- ☐ <0.5%
- ■ 0.5–0.9%
- ■ 1–1.9%
- ☐ 2–3.9%
- ■ 4–7.9%
- ■ 8–15.9%

*DALYS refers to "disability-adjusted life years." It is a measure of disease burden devised by the World Health Organization to quantify the impact of premature death and disability on a population by combining them in a single measure.

Taken from: World Health Organization, 2009.

with the rapid growth in the number of cars in many parts of the world. Fatal mass poisonings following the drinking of illegally or informally produced alcoholic beverages have been reported from several countries, but globally the public health impact of consuming non-commercially produced alcoholic beverages remains to be determined.

Harmful drinking is associated with numerous social consequences, such as crimes, violence, unemployment and absenteeism. It generates health-care and societal costs. Notwithstanding methodological problems of measurement, it represents an enormous social and economic burden: the global cost of the harmful use of alcohol in 2002 has been estimated to be between US $210,000 million and US $665,000 million. The health and social consequences tend to hurt less advantaged social groups most and contribute to disparities in health between and within countries. . . .

A Number of Strategies Can Reduce Alcohol's Harms

The public health problems caused by the harmful use of alcohol are multidimensional and complex, with significant differences in consumption levels, drinking patterns and drinking contexts between countries and regions. Various strategies and policy element options can be chosen, depending on regional circumstances, public health problems and needs of individual countries. Priority areas for action should focus on prevention of harmful drinking and should be based on the best available evidence. To be effective, strategies and policy element options should address levels, patterns and context of alcohol consumption through a combination of measures that target the population at large, vulnerable groups, such as young people and pregnant women, affected individuals and particular problems such as drink-driving and alcohol-related violence. Alcohol policies or action plans to reduce alcohol-related harm should take into account several major issues, such as the strength of evidence, cultural sensitivity, adaptation to local needs, and contexts, ensuring a sustainable and intersectoral approach, and provision for adequate monitoring and evaluation.

Raising awareness and political commitment. The actions needed to reduce harmful use of alcohol call for sustained and determined efforts by all relevant partners, as appropriate. Written alcohol policies or strategies can facilitate and clarify the contributions and division of responsibilities of the different partners who must be involved at different levels. An action plan at country and, when appropriate, subnational and municipal levels with clear objectives, strategies and targets is required. Regular reports on the harmful use of alcohol at international, national, regional and local levels need to be available to policymakers, stakeholders and a wide public audience. Building a strong base of public awareness and support can also help to secure the necessary continuity and sustainability of alcohol policies.

Health-sector response. Health-sector preventive measures against hazardous and harmful alcohol consumption, such as screening and brief interventions, have proven to be effective and cost-effective in reducing alcohol consumption and alcohol-related harm. Early identification and effective treatment in health-care settings of alcohol-use disorders, also in patients with co-morbid conditions, can reduce associated morbidity and mortality and improve the well-being of affected individuals and their families. Treatment is most effective when supported by sound policies and health systems and integrated within a broader preventive strategy. Health-care providers should concentrate on clients' health improvement and satisfaction through evidence-based and cost-effective interventions, and governments, in improving health systems, should take into consideration services for alcohol-use disorders and interventions for hazardous and harmful use of alcohol. As the main providers of health care, the many millions of health workers worldwide can contribute substantially to reducing and preventing harmful use of alcohol.

Community action to reduce the harmful use of alcohol. Community-based action, with appropriate engagement of different stakeholders, can effectively reduce the harmful use of alcohol. Community actions are particularly important in settings where unrecorded alcohol consumption is high and/or where social consequences such as public drunkenness, mistreatment of children, violence against intimate partners and sexual violence are prevalent. Community actions can increase recognition of alcohol-related harm at the community level, reduce the acceptability of public drunkenness, bolster other policy measures at the community level, enhance partnerships and networks of community agencies and nongovernmental organizations, provide care and support for affected individuals and their families, and mobilize the community against the selling and consumption of illicit and potentially contaminated alcohol.

> **FAST FACT**
>
> According to the World Health Organization, alcohol causes 1.8 million deaths worldwide each year.

Drink-driving policies and countermeasures. Strategies that aim to reduce the harm associated with drink-driving can be broadly classified as follows:

- deterrence, or direct measures that aim to reduce the likelihood of drink-driving occurring
- indirect measures that aim to reduce the likelihood of drink-driving by reducing alcohol consumption
- measures that create a safer driving environment in order to reduce the consequences and level of severity associated with impaired driver crashes.

A substantial body of research evidence exists that introducing a low limit for blood alcohol concentration reduces the harm. Young drivers are at particular risk of death from alcohol-related traffic crashes, and many countries have lowered this limit for new and/or young drivers. The success of legislation as a deterrent, and reducing the incidence of drink-driving and its consequences, largely depends on its enforcement and the severity of penalties imposed on those caught driving over the limit. Consistent enforcement by police departments using random, targeted or selective breath-testing is essential and should be supported by sustained publicity and awareness campaigns.

Addressing the availability of alcohol. Regulating production and distribution of alcoholic beverages is an effective strategy to reduce harmful use of alcohol and in particular to protect young people and other vulnerable groups. Many countries have some restrictions on the sale of alcohol. These restrictions cover the age of consumers, the type of retail establishments that can sell alcoholic beverages, and licensing, with limits on hours and days of sale and regulations on vendors and the density of outlets. However, in some developing countries the informal markets are the main source of alcohol and formal controls on sale may be of less relevance until a better system for controls and enforcement is in place.

Addressing marketing of alcoholic beverages. Young people who have chosen to drink alcoholic beverages and who drink regularly are an important market segment for alcohol producers. It is very difficult to target young adult consumers without exposing cohorts of adolescents under the legal age to the same marketing practices. Controls or partial bans on volume, placement and content of alcohol advertising are important parts of a strategy, and research results underline the need for such controls or bans, in particular to protect adolescents and young people from pressure to start drinking. Marketing practices that appeal to children and adolescents could be seen as particular policy concerns.

Pricing policies. Price is an important determinant of alcohol consumption and, in many contexts, of the extent of alcohol-related problems. Considerable evidence has accumulated to support the use of tax changes as a means of influencing price. High tax rates may not be the first choice of policy in countries where alcohol-related problems are less important or there is a considerable informal market, and interventions directed at particular subpopulations may be more cost-effective. Even in such countries, decreases in prices of alcoholic beverages or an increase in disposable income without appropriate adjustment in those prices could counteract such policies. A particular concern emerges when alcoholic drinks are cheaper than non-alcoholic alternatives such as bottled water. It is also worth keeping in mind that tax is only one component of the price of alcoholic beverages and tax changes may not always be reflected in changes in the retail price. Similarly, vendors or manufacturers may attempt to encourage demand by price promotions.

Harm reduction. Directly focusing on reducing the negative consequences of drinking and alcohol intoxication can be an effective strategy in specific contexts. A range of interventions to reduce alcohol-related harm in and around licensed premises has been developed. Interventions that focus on changing the night-life environment can reduce the harmful consequences of drinking in and around these settings, without necessarily altering overall consumption levels. The impact of these measures is greatly enhanced when there is active and ongoing enforcement of laws and regulations prohibiting sale of alcohol to intoxicated customers and policing of the streets at night. The evidence base for harm-reduction approaches, however, is not yet as well established as that for regulating the availability and demand for alcohol beverages.

Reducing the public health impact of illegally and informally produced alcohol. From a public health perspective, illegally and informally produced alcohol can create an additional negative health effect if the beverage contains methanol or other contaminants and its production and distribution are under less control than legally produced and sold alcohol. Evidence for the effectiveness of measures to counteract the public health impact of the consumption of illegally produced alcohol is weak, but points towards a combination of community mobilization and enforcement and control. The feasibility and effectiveness of countermeasures will be influenced by the fact that the purchasing power of those who buy informally produced alcohol often is extremely low. . . .

Reducing the public health problems caused by the harmful use of alcohol at the international level requires coordination and appropriate participation of different international stakeholders. Leadership is needed for building consensus around values and appropriate strategies and interventions. WHO is in a strong position to play a significant role in developing and supporting a global framework to complement regional and national actions to reduce the harmful use of alcohol.

CHAPTER 2

Controversies About Alcohol

Alcoholism Is a Disease

Jeff Miller, a conversation with Howard Fields

In the following viewpoint Jeff Miller from the University of California at San Francisco (UCSF) interviews neuroscientist Howard Fields, who believes that alcoholism is a disease. Fields hypothesizes that ill-functioning opioid receptors in alcoholics' brains may cause them to have difficulties controlling their impulses. When presented with the temptation of a drink, alcoholics cannot resist the urge, not because they do not have a strong enough moral fiber, but because they have abnormal nerve cell activity. Fields says the knowledge he and other scientists are gaining about alcoholics' brain chemistry is contributing to the development of medications that can help alcoholics control their urge to drink. Miller is the host of *Science Café*, a weekly science show at UCSF. Fields is a senior researcher at the UCSF-affiliated Ernest Gallo Clinic and Research Center.

What if we put cancer patients in jail? It's a ridiculous thought, of course. No one chooses to get cancer. It's a disease whose emergence is dictated

SOURCE: Jeff Miller, "Alcoholism: Vice or Disease? A Conversation with Howard Fields, 3 Parts," *Science Café*, April 2, 13, 19, 2007. Reproduced by permission.

Photo on facing page. One of the many controversies involving alcoholism is the debate over whether or not it is a disease. (© **Photofusion Picture Library/Alamy**)

by a complex interplay among environment, lifestyle and genetics.

Alcoholism Is a Disease, Not a Crime

Using the same logic, neuroscientist Howard Fields, MD, PhD—a senior researcher at the UCSF-affiliated Ernest Gallo Clinic and Research Center and director of UCSF's [University of California, San Francisco] Wheeler Center for the Neurobiology of Addiction—wonders, then, why we punish addicts.

"If you listen to addicts, they say, 'I'm out of control. I can't help it. I can't stop myself. I know I need help.' That's what everyone needs to understand. Most alcoholics would like to cut back on their drinking. But some unconscious force makes them take that fifth or sixth drink even when they know they shouldn't. This is a disease, not a crime."

Finding that unconscious force inside the human brain is the holy grail of Fields' research. It's a quest that has little use for the magic wand called willpower that society waves over the addiction problem as both an explanation and a solution. "Blaming a person's lack of willpower is another way of saying it's your fault, that you had a choice," says Fields. "But who chooses to be an addict? And what is willpower but just another manifestation of nerve cell activity?"

If not a failure of willpower, then, what is alcohol addiction? Fields is quick with an answer. "To me, the simplest way of thinking about it is impulsivity. In other words, if there is something immediately available, you ignore the long-term consequences. In fact, the longer term the consequences are, the less influence they will have over your current behavior. This is what we as scientists have to understand: How does your motivation for immediate reward outweigh your ability to wait for a larger pleasure?"

It's a fascinating neurobiological conundrum that all of us either witness or participate in daily. Think about it for a

Some experts say there is strong evidence that alcoholism is a disease, because alcoholics are unconsciously out of control and cannot stop themselves from drinking.
(© Phototake Inc./Alamy)

moment. At some point in our lives, almost everyone is exposed to alcohol. Yet most people do not become alcoholics, even those who drink small or moderate amounts daily.

Alcoholics Are More Impulsive than Others

For perhaps 5 percent to 10 percent of us, though, and for reasons as yet unexplained, drinking alcohol becomes an addiction with often disastrous consequences on our health, our freedom and the lives of others. The statistics are grim. In addition to the 17,000 traffic-related fatalities, alcohol abuse in the United States annually causes:

- 1,400 deaths
- 500,000 injuries
- 600,000 assaults
- 70,000 sexual assaults

What is going on inside the heads of these people? society asks with both contempt and rage. Fields has an answer of sorts. "When you compare alcoholics and controls as they decide between an immediate reward and a delayed one, you see that chronic alcoholics are much more impulsive."

Which came first, the drinking or the impulsivity? It's not an idle question, and it's one that Fields cannot yet answer. "We don't know if drinking causes impulsiveness or if innate impulsiveness makes alcoholics drink more."

Still, some of the scientific murkiness is beginning to clear. For example, Fields and his colleagues have found that for those who prefer the delayed reward, there is activity in different regions of the brain than if you prefer the immediate reward. "You can think of it as the neural correlates of the ego (immediate gratification) and superego (long-term benefit)," Fields remarks. The key point is that if there are different paths for processing immediate and delayed gratification, then the underlying neural mechanism and biochemistry must be different as well.

And if you understand these differences, you are closer to understanding what makes alcoholics different. The main point is that their brains are different, and that is why they cannot stop drinking once they start. . . .

The Opioid Receptor Theory

Kappa delta mu sounds like a college fraternity. And if you associate college with sometimes fatal outbursts of binge drinking, the Greek letters might be a fitting label.

For neuroscientists, though, kappa, delta and mu refer to opioid receptors, large molecules found on the surface of neurons. Opioids, literally "resembling opium"—which stems from the Greek word *opion*, or "poppy juice"—are a group of natural substances produced by the opium poppy plant. Similar-acting substances are also produced by the body when we are stressed or when we are anticipating reward. Think endorphins. . . .

Fields . . . believes that small differences in receptor activity might be a major culprit in alcoholism. . . .

"I want to be clear, though," Fields adds. "Higher degrees of impulsivity [the genetics of which are still being worked out] seem to be a risk factor for alcoholism. But if you grow up in a Mormon community where there is strong pressure against drinking alcohol, you probably will not become an alcoholic. Take that same person, though, and put him or her in an environment where there is a lot of stress and people are relieving their anxiety by drinking, and the results might be very different. We have to always remember that there are a lot of reasons why people drink."

And a lot of theories. Fields acknowledges that the opioid receptor hypothesis is only one of many, and none are yet proven. In addition to opioids, some scientists favor the GABA receptor theory; GABA, short for gamma-amino butyric acid, is a neurotransmitter, a substance that governs how electrical signals pass between cells.

"There are some scientists," says Fields, "who think alcohol is addicting primarily through a direct action on GABA receptors that indirectly activates dopamine neurons. It's true that alcohol does produce an increase in dopamine concentration in the brain, where we know that feelings of reward originate. And we know that rats bred to like alcohol will choose a lever to deliver alcohol directly into the region of their brains where there are dopamine neurons."

Alcoholism May Be a Failure to Know When "Enough Is Enough"

Yet there is another principle at work that Fields finds equally fascinating. It involves satiety, or—more accurately—the failure of satiety to literally signal "enough is enough."

"When we eat, we eventually get full, and eating is no longer pleasant. That's the satiety mechanism at work. What if alcoholism is a failure of satiety? What if alcoholics keep drinking because they never feel like they've had enough? Maybe alcohol is handled a lot like food."

Animal models reveal that endorphins acting at the mu subtype of opioid receptor promote eating and suppress satiety. Conversely, endorphins activating the kappa receptor promote satiety. So what about the endorphins released in the brain when someone drinks alcohol? Where do they go?

That's what Fields and his colleagues are trying to nail down. Questions abound. "Are there equal numbers of receptors?" he asks. "Do different endogenous opioids act on mu and kappa receptors? Is the balance between a mu receptor that promotes drinking and a kappa receptor that suppresses drinking at least partially responsible for how much you drink?"

Using Medications to Treat Alcohol Addiction

The answers might finally pinpoint where exactly alcohol acts to produce its powerful sense of reward. That region—or the molecular activity within it—then becomes a potential drug target. In Fields' mind, it boils down to this: "What we're doing in my lab is using animals to find out what would be the ideal combination of receptor agonists and antagonists to maximally reduce drinking, then try to design a molecule that would have those properties."

For now, naltrexone remains one of the few drugs effective for treating alcohol addiction. The operative word here is "treat," not cure. Still, if you ask law enforcement and probation officials in Butte County, California, what they think about naltrexone treatment for alcohol abusers, particularly repeat offenders tempted to get behind the wheel again, the answer would likely be applause. Indeed, the latest figures show a 30 percent drop in recidivism among those required to take the drug.

"Naltrexone is effective," says Fields. "It reduces the amount you will drink, which means that for many people, it's the difference between two drinks and five drinks. But getting people to stay on it is tough. And it might not work for everyone, maybe because it blocks both the delta and kappa receptors. Activated kappa receptors suppress alcohol intake. So if you block them, like what some have done in animal studies, you could be creating conditions where some people drink more while taking naltrexone instead of less."

Another drug, called rimonabant (Acomplia), now being sold in various European countries as an anti-obesity drug, also seems to reduce both cigarette smoking and alcohol intake, although its increased risk of depression has made the US Food and Drug Administration wary. Nonetheless, if approved, rimonabant's off-label use could rival its primary purpose.

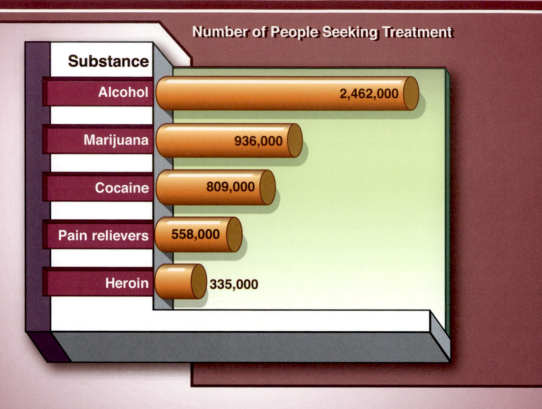

Number of People Seeking Treatment

Substance	
Alcohol	2,462,000
Marijuana	936,000
Cocaine	809,000
Pain relievers	558,000
Heroin	335,000

Taken from: Substance Abuse and Mental Health Services Administration, Office of Applied Studies, National Survey on Drug Use and Health, 2006 and 2007.

Fields wouldn't mind the competition. "Based on the research going on here and other places in the US and around the world, I would say that in the next five to 10 years, addiction treatment is going to be markedly improved by the introduction of new pharmacological agents." . . .

Treatment Programs Resistant to Using Medications

"Most treatment programs for alcoholics don't use a lot of medication," he says. "They use detoxification and cognitive behavioral transformation, like the 12 Steps of Alcoholics Anonymous (AA). This is fine. Many people are helped, but relapse is very common. What I'd like to see is more clinical research. The biggest hurdle is that not everyone in the medical profession has yet to buy into the fact that addiction is really a disease of the nervous system. It's exciting, of course, that all the science is inevitably going to lead to some new treatments. And I think that after one or two truly effective drugs come along, people's attitudes toward alcoholism will change just like they did about depression when antidepressants came out. But," he adds, "what good is a new medication if the treatment community doesn't want to use it?" . . .

In short, says Fields, there are many in the treatment community who resist using medications. Their rationalization? "Another drug is just another crutch."

Is their criticism far? Some would argue yes. Since addiction is known to hijack the pleasure centers of the brain, replacing this destructive high with an elevated—some might say "spiritual"—one puts personal rehabilitation rather than biomedical intervention at the center of the treatment universe.

AA's 12-Step Program Can Help Some Addicts

And there is evidence that this approach has merit, at least for some. For example, a 2003 study of 722 AA members revealed that those who were encouraged by fellow members to stop drinking were three times more likely to be abstinent after a year than those who received no support at all. More interesting, if the encouragement came from non-AA members, the impact on abstinence was negligible.

Does this mean that the vigilance and "self awakening" inherent in AA's 12-Step therapy (TS) is a cure in itself? No. When it comes to addiction, cure is a big and misleading word. The brain simply "learns" to like addictive substances too much, even filing away a menu of environmental triggers—a street corner, money, a sound, a smell—to [cue] up the urge. In short, abstinence is a daily battle.

So what to make of other studies confirming that TS therapy can be superior to cognitive behavioral therapy "when total abstinence is the desired outcome"? Does this prove the case for moral fiber? After all, if some addicts can control the urge to abuse drugs or drink excessively without relying on any anti-addiction drugs, isn't this a victory of the will?

Fields, ever the neuroscientist, thinks not. "In my mind, any change in behavior is secondary to a change in the brain. Will power does exist, but it is biologically based and can be influenced by drugs for better or worse. If drugs can dissolve your will power, it follows that other drugs can restore it." Still, as the TS study suggests, something very human—if as yet uncharted in the brain—can contribute to sustained behavioral change.

> **FAST FACT**
>
> More than 19 million people needed treatment for an alcohol problem during 2007, according to the National Survey on Drug Use and Health.

Treatment Instead of Jail

The same can be said of the criminal justice system, Fields answers. Effective does not always mean scientifically enlightened. "If your attitude is that addiction should be punished because some drugs are illegal and it's a crime to take them, that's one approach. When you choose that approach, you are also saying that people are moral individuals, that people are responsible for their actions, that if someone chooses to do something that society does not approve of, then that person should be punished and that the punishment is a disincentive for other people to engage in the same behavior. It works up to a point. Look at Prohibition. Rates of alcoholism went way down. There's no question that making some drugs illegal does discourage many people from taking them."

The problem as Fields sees it is that criminalizing addiction is a half measure with a dead end. "If your attitude, like mine, is that addiction is an illness, you don't put people in jail. Instead you find ways to get them treated because you want to solve the problem, not just reduce it."

And on that last point, alone, all would agree.

Alcoholism Is Not a Disease

Baldwin Research Institute

In the following viewpoint the Baldwin Research Institute (BRI) contends that alcoholism is a choice, not a disease. The BRI says that the premise that alcoholism is a disease is based on fraud and greed. According to the BRI, three influential but dubious characters from the twentieth century were able to convince the medical community to proclaim that alcoholism is a disease. Since then, says the BRI, the disease concept of alcoholism has been perpetuated by Alcoholics Anonymous and other 12-step programs. The BRI believes that labeling alcoholism as a disease removes any personal responsibility alcoholics may feel toward trying to quit and keeps them bound in their addiction. However, acknowledging that alcoholism is a choice empowers alcoholics to use self-control and makes it more likely that they can shake the shackles of their addiction. The Baldwin Research Institute is a New York–based nonprofit organization whose mission involves researching and developing programs for recovery from drug and alcohol problems.

SOURCE: "Alcoholism: A Disease of Speculation," Baldwin Research Institute, 2003. Copyright © 2003 Baldwin Research Institute. Reproduced by permission.

"In 1976, the writer Ivan Illich warned in the book, *Limits to Medicine*, that 'the medical establishment has become a major threat to health.' At the time, he was dismissed as a maverick, but a quarter of a century later, even the medical establishment is prepared to admit that he may well be right. (Anthony Browne, April 14, 2002, *The Observer*)"

The Disease Concept's Dubious Beginnings

History and science have shown us that the existence of the disease of alcoholism is pure speculation. Just saying alcoholism is a disease, doesn't make it true. Nevertheless, medical professionals and American culture lovingly embraced the disease concept and quickly applied it to every possible deviant behavior from alcohol abuse to compulsive lecturing. The disease concept was a panacea for many failing medical institutions adding billions of dollars to the industry and leading to a prompt evolution of pop-psychology. Research has shown that alcoholism is a choice, not a disease, and stripping alcohol abusers of their choice, by applying the disease concept, is a threat to the health of the individual.

The disease concept oozes into every crevice of our society perpetuating harmful misinformation that hurts the very people it was intended to help. It is a backwards situation where the assumptions of a few were adopted as fact by the medical profession, devoid of supporting evidence. And soon after, the disease concept was accepted by the general public. With this said, visiting the history of the disease concept gives us all a better understanding of how and why all of this happened.

The disease concept originated in the 1800s with a fellow by the name of Dr. Benjamin Rush. He believed alcoholics were diseased and used the idea to promote his prohibitionist political platform. He also believed that dishonesty,

The Baldwin Research Institute maintains that alcoholism is not a disease but a choice, and acknowledging that it is a choice can lead alcoholics to recovery. (© Collective/Alamy)

political dissension and being of African-American descent were diseases. The "disease concept" was used throughout the late 1800s and early 1900s by prohibitionists and those involved in the Temperance Movement to further a political agenda. Prior to this time, the term alcoholic did not exist. Alcohol was freely consumed, but drunkenness was not tolerated. Many sociologists contribute its non-existence to the very stigma that the disease concept removes. . . . During this period of time social ties and family played a much more influential role in an individual's life. Therefore, deviant behaviors were undesirable and less likely to occur. It was not until industrialization began, when the importance of social and family ties diminished, that alcoholism became a problem. We now live in a society that encourages binge drinking as a social norm, but at the same time, we live in a society that discourages it.

The "recovery" community's adoption of the disease concept began with an early AA [Alcoholics Anonymous] member named Marty Mann. Her efforts, combined with a somewhat dubious scientist named E.M. Jellinek, began national acceptance of the disease concept. It was Jellinek's "scientific" study that opened the door for the medical communities' support. E.M. Jellinek's study was funded by the efforts of Marty Mann and R. Brinkley Smithers. And, like so many other circumstances involving Jellinek and Marty Mann, the study was bogus if not outright fraudulent. The surveys he based his conclusions on were from a hand picked group of alcoholics. There were 158 questionnaires handed out and 60 of them were suspiciously not included. His conclusion was based on less than 100 hand picked alcoholics chosen by Marty Mann. Ms. Mann, of course, had a personal agenda to remove the stigma about the homeless and dirty alcoholic or "bowery drunk" in order to gain financial support from the wealthy. By removing the stigma, the problem becomes one of the general population, which would then include the wealthy. The first step was Jellinek publishing his findings in his book *The Stages of Alcoholism*, which was based on the selective study. Later, E.M. Jellinek was asked by Yale University to refute his own findings. He complied. E.M. Jellinek's *Stages of Alcoholism* did not stand up to scientific scrutiny.

AMA's Self-Seeking and Shady Proclamations

Early in the 20th Century, the validity of the disease concept was often debated in medical circles. However, in 1956 the American Medical Association (AMA) proclaimed alcoholism an "illness." Then, in 1966, the AMA proclaimed alcoholism a disease. The decision was wrapped in controversy. Historically, Marty Mann had her hand in much of this and manipulated information and doctors into agreeing with the disease concept. Marty Mann used her position as founder of the NCA (National Coun[cil] for Alcoholism) to promote the disease concept through Jellinek and a somewhat clandestine relationship with the founder of the NIAAA [National Institute on Alcohol Abuse and Alcoholism] whose founder worked with Marty Mann during the institute's early development. The founder of NIAAA (R. Brinkley Smithers) was a major contributor to and promoter of the disease concept. It was his money that actually funded Jellinek's work at Yale. Smithers was also responsible for gaining insurance coverage for patients in treatment (hence the 28 day program). Smithers was certainly not altruistic in his efforts. At that time he had already launched a treatment program for which he was lobbying for insurance payments. Acceptance by the medical community was the only way this could happen; alcoholism had to be a medical problem in order for medical insurance to pay for programs. We can see the influence of these "advances" everyday in treatment programs. Today the treatment industry is a multi-billion dollar industry, with insurance paying the lion's share of the costs. . . .

While many advocate for its benefits, the disease concept has proven to be far more damaging to the substance abuser then anyone could have predicted. Therapists claim the disease concept helps the patient to understand the seriousness of [his/her] problems. But in reality, this idea has backfired. The disease concept strips the substance abuser of responsibility. A disease cannot be cured by force of will; therefore, adding the medical label transfers the responsibility from the abuser to caregivers. Inevitably the abusers become unwilling victims, and just as inevitably they take on that role. In retrospect then, the disease concept has effectively increased alcoholism and drug abuse. Furthermore, its only benefit has been vast monetary reward for the professionals and governmental agencies responsible for providing recovery services. Specifically, it has not offered a solution for those attempting to stop abusive alcohol and drug use. . . .

In a recent Gallup poll, 90 percent of people surveyed believe that alcoholism is a disease. Most argue that because the American Medical Association (AMA) has proclaimed alcoholism a disease, the idea is without reproach. But, the fact is that the AMA made this determination in the absence of empirical evidence. After reviewing the history of the decision, it would not be unreasonable to suggest that the AMA has been pursuing its own agenda in the face of evidence negating the validity of alcoholism. While the AMA has made extraordinary contributions in the mental health field, it is not outside the box. The AMA is a part of the capitalist paradigm that is necessary for our society to function. The promulgation of the disease concept, in conjunction with AMA approval, has created a multi-billion dollar treatment industry that contributes billions to the health care industry. But, even with the AMA's lofty status, mistakes in classifications can and have resulted in disastrous consequence.

The Classification of Diseases

While the AMA's classifications for the most part are accurate, the organization is not without error. Since its inception the AMA has made classifications of varying "deviant" behaviors without scientific research to validate its claims. And, for whatever reason, the definition of a disease, as set forth by the AMA, is a malleable and all inclusive definition allowing for the inclusion of almost every behavior, deviant or otherwise. As a result, every unwanted behavior can be medicalized and medically treated thereby providing professionals with more patients and more income.

With respect to alcoholism, it is beyond the grasp of logic for medical professionals to prescribe 12-Step type meeting attendance as a remedy for an "incurable" medical ailment, not to mention a contradiction to the supposed nature of the problem. Medical professionals are admittedly incapable of helping drug addicts and alcoholics so they pass the buck to organizations outside of the medical community. But, because of recidivism rates and treatment failure, the buck is passed right back. . . . After an array of varying forms of "therapy" the patient is released with a prescription for lifelong attendance to AA or NA [Narcotics Anonymous] meetings. . . .

The absurdities do not stop with 12 Step groups; professionals contribute their own set of absurdities. For example, the AMA's definition of alcoholism is: "Alcoholism is an illness characterized by preoccupation with alcohol and loss of control over its consumption, such as to lead usually to intoxication if drinking; by chronicity, by progression and by a tendency toward relapse. It is typically associated with physical disability and impaired emotional, occupational and/or social adjustments as a direct consequence of persistent excessive use."

A natural assumption would be that the classification of a disease requires that characteristics and symptoms can be measured or observed. While the majority of diseases fit this requirement, substance abuse does not. The contradiction to these requirements lies within the defined nature of "alcoholism." This supposed disease's symptoms are only discovered after the consumption of alcohol. The health risks, dangerous behaviors and repercussions only materialize after the alcohol is consumed and *not before*. In comparison, the diagnosis for cancer comes after symptoms surface or cancerous cells are discovered. There are

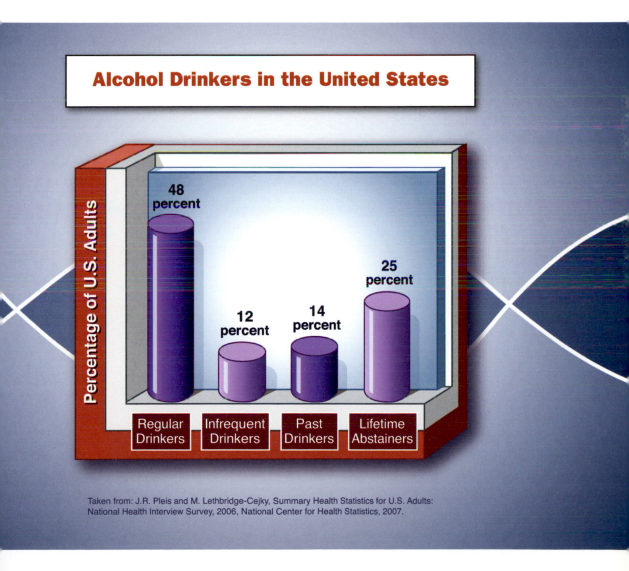

Alcohol Drinkers in the United States

Taken from: J.R. Pleis and M. Lethbridge-Cejky, Summary Health Statistics for U.S. Adults: National Health Interview Survey, 2006, National Center for Health Statistics, 2007.

physically visible anomalies that can be measured. This measurement does not exist with alcoholics. The majority of time, the diagnosis of alcoholism is a guess, if indeed such a diagnosis actually exists. There is little question that a person exposed to enough carcinogens or radiation will eventually get cancer. With alcohol it is questionable if a person will become a problem drinker if exposed to alcohol. While cancer is a separate entity of its own within the body that first exists without the knowledge of its host, overconsumption of alcohol, a substance consumed by choice, is necessary before a diagnosis can be made. That is to say that one must choose to create the condition before the condition can exist and subsequently be diagnosed. . . .

Sociologists and psychologists have long since been aware of the dangers of medicalising deviant behaviors. Most encourage extreme caution when diagnosing mental illness because of the potential for damage in doing so. People who are labeled usually conform to the standards that the label calls for whether the diagnosis is correct or not. It's dangerous ground that is commonly tread upon by professionals today.

What's even more disheartening is that a large percentage of diagnoses are not made by doctors, but by unqualified "drug counselors." Treatment and AA are recommended by counselors as a way to "nip it in the bud" but these recommendations do far more damage to the individual than if they had just been left alone. . . . It should be pointed out that there is a major conflict of interest among drug counselors, a conflict of interest that cannot be ignored. The majority are, themselves, members of 12 step groups and are believers in AA dogma. These non-professional "professional" counselors have been manipulated into believing 12-Step propaganda. And, like the AMA, their "profes-

FAST FACT

According to the Centers for Disease Control and Prevention, excessive alcohol use is the third leading lifestyle-related cause of death for people in the United States each year.

sional" status allows counselors to convince their patients that the patients need help because they are sick.

The Absurdity of a Genetic Link for Alcoholism

And, if this 12 Step nonsense is not harmful enough, misinformation abounds. Consider that recently in an attempt to prove a genetic link for alcohol and drug abuse, most studies only provide roundabout evidence of a predisposition, not a cause for alcoholism. With this said, we should point out that the predisposition can only prove a difference in bodily processes, *not a difference in thinking*. "Knowing the sequence of individual genes doesn't tell you anything about the complexities of what life is," said Dr. Brian Goodwin, a theoretical biologist at Schumacher College in Devon, England, and a member of the Santa Fe Institute in New Mexico. Goodwin goes on to explain [that] single gene mutations are not accountable for, and cannot explain, complex behaviors. Genes produce proteins, they do not guide behaviors. The truth is a predisposition for substance abuse, if it does exist, has no bearing on subsequent behaviors. Chemical processes do not make a person an alcoholic. The person makes the conscious choice. Altered processing of alcohol in no way determines choice or behaviors. Obsessive drinking is not a reaction to bodily processes, but merely a choice. The amount consumed is determined by the individual not by the body.

Nevertheless, news stories surface every year proclaiming discoveries of the genetic sources of emotional and behavioral problems while ignoring the mountains of evidence that refutes such preposterous assertions. Genetics is the new panacea for medical professionals. Since 1987 such reports have appeared on the front page of the *New York Times* in connection with manic-depressive disorder, schizophrenia, homosexuality, drug abuse and alcoholism. . . .

Looking at the situation objectively, if alcoholism is passed through genes, the abnormality must be relatively new. As stated previously, alcoholism did not exist in the early colonization of America. In fact, it did not exist until the late 1700's. Some would argue that the residents of the United States are largely immigrants and as a result the alcoholism gene was introduced later in history. Meaning, the "new" citizens are not of the same family tree as those of the 1700s. But, it's important to point out, many cultures outside of the United States do not even know what alcoholism is; they do not have a word for it. People with different cultural backgrounds do not have different genetic make-ups. America's arrogance has led the population to believe that we are scientifically more advanced than other cultures; therefore, we know the truth and they do not. But this is far from true. In a country where we claim to "know the truth," the city of Los Angeles has more addicts than all of Europe. While professionals strive to remove the stigma surrounding alcoholics, they are in essence, removing the social unacceptability of the act. By removing the stigma, they are encouraging this socially unacceptable behavior to continue. We replaced the negative stigma with positive acceptance.

Today the AMA reports that while there is no "alcoholic personality," it does not seem unreasonable to believe that there may be "some combination of personality traits which are contributive to the development of alcoholism." They assert that emotional immaturity and strong dependency needs are commonly seen in alcoholics. While researchers work hard to prove the disease concept sound and verifiable, repeated studies refute the impact of genetic predispositions. [Psychologist Stanton Peele notes,] "A great deal of evidence, more consistent and extensive than anything yet established by biological research, shows that social categories are the best predictors of drinking problems and alcoholism." . . .

Alcoholics Anonymous's Success Is Society's Failure

Irrefutable empirical evidence has shown that organizations and institutions [that] promote, and adhere to, the disease concept, fail when trying to help people with substance abuse problems. Alcoholics Anonymous has successfully promoted itself as the only hope for alcohol abusers. The public perception is that Alcoholics Anonymous works, but the reality is something completely different.

In 65 years Alcoholics Anonymous has become a part of our social structure. Its tenets have led the medical establishment and been used to diagnose patients with alcoholism while simultaneously giving birth to dozens of spin-off anonymous meetings. Its most outstanding accomplishment has been successfully promoting a fictitious disease as fact, and to be absorbed into the very fabric of our society. But, while Alcoholics Anonymous has accomplished the unthinkable, its accomplishments have damaged the society. Although its intentions are synonymous with help, the organization's lies and manipulations have damaged society as a whole, costing taxpayers billions of dollars and costing families the lives of their loved ones. . . .

Repeated studies have shown that the average person, who could be diagnosed with a substance abuse problem, will discontinue use *on their own* 20 to 30 percent of the time. But, those who are exposed to AA and treatment and who are taught the disease concept have a drastically decreased chance of achieving sobriety. While treatment professionals are aware of program failure, governing organizations support and promote the adoption of 12 Step tenets into treatment programs for substance abusers. Families pay tens of thousands of dollars to help their loved ones only to place them in programs that follow guidelines of another failing program. Any program based on a program that fails will inevitably fail. For most, 12 Step has become synonymous with failure.

Giving People Back Their Ability to Choose

In contrast, programs that teach control and choice are far more successful than programs that teach the disease concept. While conventional treatment methods result in a 3 percent success rate after five years, programs that do not teach the disease concept, and instead teach choice, have success rates of 86 percent after five and even 10 years.

In conclusion, after reviewing the available research from both sides of the debate, the belief in the disease of alcoholism, creates the existence of the disease. Organizations and institutions that promote the disease concept are, in many cases, doing irreparable harm to the individual and performing a disservice to the population as a whole. Geneticists are aware that a predisposition does not dictate subsequent behavior, and treatment professionals are aware that the programs they offer fail. It is an outright injustice when faced with the facts. Stripping human beings of their ability to choose is damaging, whereas giving them back the power of their own volition is essential for recovery. Alcoholism is a choice, not a disease.

Drinking on College Campuses Is a Serious Problem

National Center on Addiction and Substance Abuse at Columbia University

In the following viewpoint the National Center on Addiction and Substance Abuse (CASA) asserts that substance abuse is rampant on college campuses and alcohol is the main substance abused. According to CASA, college alcohol abuse has not gotten any better since it was identified as a problem in the early 1990s. Binge drinking, defined as consuming four (by women) or five (by men) drinks in a row, and other risky drinking behaviors have gotten worse, says CASA. The organization identifies several consequences of alcohol abuse at colleges, including failing grades, injuries, drunk driving, and sexual promiscuity. CASA says college administrators, parents, and the alcohol industry contribute to the problem by enabling a culture of drinking and drugs. CASA is a national organization located at Columbia University that studies and seeks to prevent alcohol and substance abuse in all sectors of American society.

SOURCE: *Wasting the Best and the Brightest: Substance Abuse at America's Colleges and Universities,* New York: The National Center on Addiction and Substance Abuse at Columbia University, 2007. Copyright © 2007. All rights reserved. Reproduced by permission.

In 1993 and 1994, The National Center on Addiction and Substance Abuse (CASA) at Columbia University released its first reports on substance abuse at America's colleges and universities. These reports drew attention to the widespread problems of student smoking and drinking, and highlighted the escalating problem of dangerous drinking among college women. More than a decade later, CASA's exhaustive examination of the current situation reveals an intensified student culture of abuse of addictive substances in colleges and universities across America and a range of harmful academic, health and social consequences that extend into the surrounding communities.

Alcohol Is the Main Drug in a Culture of Abuse

The main drug of abuse on college campuses remains alcohol. Unfortunately, the proportion of students who drink today has remained high (between 65 and 70 percent) since the early 1990s. Of even greater concern, students who drink and binge drink now are more likely to do so frequently, become intoxicated and drink just to get drunk than students more than a decade ago.

But the drug abuse problem goes far beyond alcohol. Since the early 1990s, the proportion of students abusing controlled prescription drugs has exploded: abuse of painkillers like Percocet, Vicodin and OxyContin has increased by more than 300 percent and abuse of stimulants like Ritalin and Adderall is up more than 90 percent. The proportion of students who are daily marijuana users has increased 110 percent. The percent using drugs like cocaine and heroin is on the rise as well.

This culture of abuse is taking its toll in student accidents, assaults, property damage, academic problems, illnesses, injuries, mental health problems, risky sex, rape and deaths.

Alcohol Abusers Also Abuse Prescription Drugs

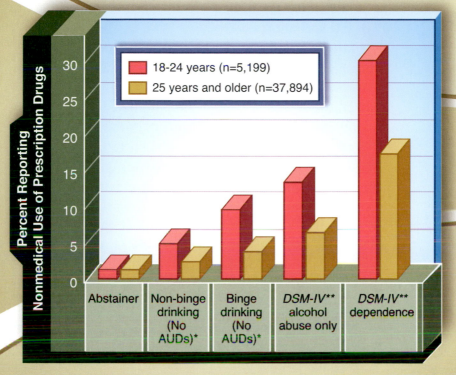

Legend:
- 18-24 years (n=5,199)
- 25 years and older (n=37,894)

Y-axis: Percent Reporting Nonmedical Use of Prescription Drugs (0, 5, 10, 15, 20, 25, 30)

X-axis categories: Abstainer, Non-binge drinking (No AUDs)*, Binge drinking (No AUDs)*, DSM-IV** alcohol abuse only, DSM-IV** dependence

* AUD: Alcohol Use Disorder
**DSM-IV: Diagnostic and Statistical Manual of Mental Disorders, 4th edition

Taken from: Elizabeth Ashton, "Alcohol Abuse Makes Prescription Drug Abuse More Likely," *NIDA Notes*, National Institute on Drug Abuse, March 2008.

Alcohol and Drug Abuse Are Enabled

Students turn to alcohol or prescription drugs to relieve stress, improve mood or enhance performance. Alcohol and tobacco companies and retailers aggressively market their products to young people. Alumni set bad examples by excessive drinking at campus homecomings and athletic events. Trustees choose not to examine the nature and extent of substance abuse among students and not to demand action to address it. And, parents may enable student drinking and other drug use by paying for it, supplying alcohol and prescription drugs, simply choosing to look the other way when their children start drinking or using other drugs in high school, and underwriting substance-fueled occasions like spring break.

In the face of this widespread enabling behavior, many college administrators shy away from drawing attention to the problem or cracking down on this culture of abuse. This failure to act has led some parents and students to seek redress in the courts for injuries and deaths.

Research has shown what it will take to face this problem: strong administrative leadership; comprehensive campus-community prevention, intervention and enforcement; controls on advertising and marketing of alcohol and tobacco; and parental engagement. But we have not yet mustered the collective will to act. Meanwhile, the college culture of abuse worsens and threatens the health and future of some of our most promising young adults. . . .

A Call to Action

Amid this college culture of substance abuse, only one-fifth of college and university administrators say their schools bear primary responsibility to prevent substance abuse among students. Two-thirds say that responsibility belongs to students. . . .

Institutions of higher education have an obligation to take on the problem of student drinking, smoking and other drug use and abuse for three primary reasons:

Student substance abuse comprises academic performance. Continuing to pass such behavior off as a harmless rite of passage and subtly condoning it—for example, by canceling Friday classes or allowing on-campus student bars—place institutions of higher learning in jeopardy of failing to achieve desired standards of academic excellence.

Educational institutions have a public health obligation to protect students, faculty and administrators from exposure to smoking and from alcohol and drug abuse, just as they would protect them from exposure to environmental toxins such as asbestos, lead or radon, or to other dangerous or unhealthy living conditions. They cannot ignore this obligation, given the compelling and growing body of evidence of the devastating health and social consequences of use and abuse of these drugs—both to the students who use them and to those around them.

Substance abuse has significant legal implications. First, it is against the law for students under age 21 to drink and for any student to use illicit drugs or take controlled prescription drugs without a valid doctor's order. Second, school failure to employ comprehensive evidence-based practices to prevent student alcohol and other drug abuse places colleges and universities at increasing risk for liability lawsuits potentially costing millions of dollars as parents and students seek redress for the damages, including wrongful death from alcohol poisoning or accidents, caused by substance abuse at colleges and universities.

The need for leadership extends beyond college and university administrators to faculty and staff, trustees, alumni, parents, students and policymakers.

Studying Alcohol and Drug Abuse at Colleges

More than a decade ago, CASA convened its landmark *Commission on Substance Abuse at Colleges and Universities* to understand better the issues surrounding substance abuse at our nation's colleges and universities. The *Commission* issued two reports: *The Smoke-Free Campus: A Report by the Commission on Substance Abuse at Colleges and Universities* (1993) and *Rethinking Rites of Passage: Substance Abuse on America's Campuses* (1994).

In 2002, CASA reconvened and expanded the *Commission on Substance Abuse at Colleges and Universities II*, again chaired by Reverend Edward (Monk) Malloy, now President Emeritus, University of Notre Dame. Using the findings from our original research in this area as a backdrop, over the past four years CASA, with guidance from the *Commission,* has conducted a comprehensive analysis to examine what progress, if any, has been made and to determine what can be done to reduce alcohol, tobacco and other drug use among college students.

CASA's analysis included a nationally representative telephone survey of 2,000 students; surveys of approximately 400 college and university administrators; extensive in-depth analyses of six national data sets; interviews with key researchers and other leaders in the field; eight focus groups; and a review of approximately 800 articles.

The Size and Shape of the Alcohol Problem

From 1993 to 2005, there has been no significant reduction in the levels of drinking and binge drinking among college students. In 2005, 67.9 percent of students (approximately 5.3 million students) reported drinking in the past month and 40.1 percent (approximately 3.1 million students) reported binge drinking. However, from 1993 to 2001 rates of riskier drinking—frequent binge drinking —being intoxicated, drinking to get drunk—have increased.

The proportion of students reporting frequent binge drinking increased 15.7 percent (from 19.7 percent to 22.8 percent). Other indicators of increased risky drinking showed even greater increases over that period: a 24.9 percent increase in drinking on 10 or more occasions in the past month (18.1 percent to 22.6 percent); a 25.6 percent increase in being intoxicated three or more times in the past month (23.4 percent to 29.4 percent); and a 20.8 percent increase in drinking for the purpose of getting drunk in the past month (39.9 percent to 48.2 percent). . . .

In 2005, 69.0 percent or 3.4 million full-time college students reported drinking, abusing controlled prescription drugs, using illicit drugs or smoking in the past month; 49.4 percent or 3.8 million reported binge drinking, abusing controlled prescription drugs or using illicit drugs in the past month. Almost one-half (45 percent or 2.3 million) of those who drink engage in two or more other forms of substance use (binge drinking, illicit drug use, prescription drug abuse or smoking).

When definitions of binge drinking are adjusted for differences in female physiology, virtually the same proportion of male and female students binge drink on a typical drinking occasion. The relative increase between 1993 and 2001 in frequent binge drinking, being drunk three

According to the National Center on Addiction and Substance Abuse, binge drinking on college campuses is an accelerating problem. (MCT/Landov)

or more times and drinking on 10 or more occasions in the past 30 days was greater for college women than it was for college men. Rates of controlled prescription drug abuse and illicit drug use increased more sharply for college men than for college women between 1993 and 2005. College women are somewhat likelier than college men to be daily smokers and daily heavy smokers.

White students are likelier to use and abuse all forms of drugs than are minority students. Students attending historically black colleges and universities (HBCUs)—regardless of their race/ethnicity—use all forms of substances at much lower rates than other students.

Harmful Consequences

The harmful consequences linked to college student substance abuse are on the rise. There is no one data source for these consequences so CASA has assembled the best and most up to date information available from a variety of sources.

Between 1993 and 2001, there has been a 37.6 percent increase in the proportion of college students hurt or injured as a result of their alcohol use (9.3 percent vs. 12.8 percent). In 2001, 1,717 college students died from unintentional alcohol-related injuries—up six percent from 1998.

Compared to 22 other countries, college students in the U.S. who drive have the highest rate of drinking and driving (50 percent of male drinkers and 35 percent of female drinkers). In 1993, 26.6 percent of college students drove under the influence of alcohol; in 2001 29 percent did so.

The average number of alcohol-related arrests per campus increased 21 percent between 2001 and 2005. In 2005, alcohol-related arrests constituted 83 percent of campus arrests.

When drunk or high, college students are more likely to be sexually active and to have sex with someone they just met. More than three-fourths (78 percent) of college students who have used illicit drugs have had sexual intercourse compared to 44 percent of those who never used drugs. In 1993, 19.2 percent of college students who used alcohol in the past year reported engaging in alcohol-related unplanned sexual activity; in 2001, 21.3 percent of student drinkers did so.

The most common secondary effects of college student drinking are property damage and vandalism, fights, rape and other sexual violence and disruption to other students' quality of life. Financial costs include damage to campus property, increase in security staff and counselors, lost tuition from dropouts and legal costs of suits against the college for liability. Residents living within a mile of college campuses report more incidents of public drunkenness, drug use, crime, vandalism and loitering than those living more than a mile away.

Young people who report current alcohol use give significantly lower ratings of their own health than do alcohol abstainers or past users. Depression, anxiety and personality disturbances in young adulthood are associated with marijuana and other illicit drug use during the teen years. In recent years, there has been a sharp increase in the number of students in need of mental health services. Young smokers are three times more likely than non-smokers to have consulted a doctor or mental health professional because of emotional or psychological problems and almost twice as likely to develop symptoms of depression.

> **FAST FACT**
>
> According to the National Institute on Alcohol Abuse and Alcoholism, each year alcohol contributes to 599,000 injuries, 696,000 assaults, and 97,000 incidents of sexual abuse of college-age people.

College students who report seriously having considered attempting suicide in the past 12 months are likelier than other students to engage in current binge drinking (41.9 percent vs. 39.6 percent), marijuana use (23.2 percent vs. 16.1 percent), other illicit drug use (6.7 percent vs. 2.8 percent), and smoking (31.9 percent vs.

19.9 percent), even after taking into consideration age, gender and race.

Student drinking and drug use are linked to lower grade point averages (GPA). Drinking impairs learning, memory, abstract thinking, problem solving and perceptual motor skills (such as eye-hand coordination). More than five percent of binge-drinking students report having been suspended; 50.6 percent have gotten behind in their schoolwork and 68.1 percent report missing classes. Alcohol and drug law violations by students also can mar their academic and legal records, compromising their career options.

Large Numbers of College Students Are Alcoholics

Almost one in four (22.9 percent or 1.8 million) full-time college students already meet the *DSM-IV* [*Diagnostic and Statistical Manual of Mental Disorders,* 4th edition] diagnostic criteria for alcohol and/or drug abuse (12.3 percent for alcohol abuse; 2.5 percent for drug abuse) or alcohol and/or drug dependence (7.7 percent for alcohol dependence, 4.7 percent for drug dependence) in the past year. This is compared to less than one in 10 (8.5 percent) in the general population who meet the *DSM-IV* diagnostic criteria for alcohol and/or drug abuse or dependence.

College Drinking Is Exaggerated

Aaron M. White

In the following viewpoint Aaron M. White contends that although college student drinking is a serious problem, it is not an epidemic. According to White, most people, college students included, think that college drinking is an epidemic because the idea has been perpetuated by the media. Movies and news stories tend to portray college life as one big drinking event. However, White says, when one looks closely at the data, it becomes apparent that college drinking may not be as pervasive as the media portrays it to be. For instance, says White, although the number of binge drinking college students has increased, so too has the number of abstaining college students. According to White, some college students do have a drinking problem, but most college students do not. White is an assistant professor at Duke University's Department of Psychiatry.

Alcohol use among college students has been a topic of intense interest in recent years. Without question, excessive use of alcohol is associated with a

SOURCE: Aaron M. White, "College-Drinking," *Topics in Alcohol Research*, 2004. Reproduced by permission.

wide range of deleterious outcomes among students. It is well known that heavy drinking increases the likelihood of committing a litany of crimes, including vandalism and physical assault, and non-drinkers routinely suffer the consequences of other students' irresponsible drinking. [Researchers have found] the more a student drinks the lower their overall GPA [grade point average] is likely to be. More than 1/2 of students in one nationwide survey report having their studying or sleep disrupted by someone else's alcohol use. In addition, as in the larger population, drinking and driving is a problem on many campuses. Traffic crashes claim more lives than anything else among young adults, and alcohol is involved in a significant proportion of these

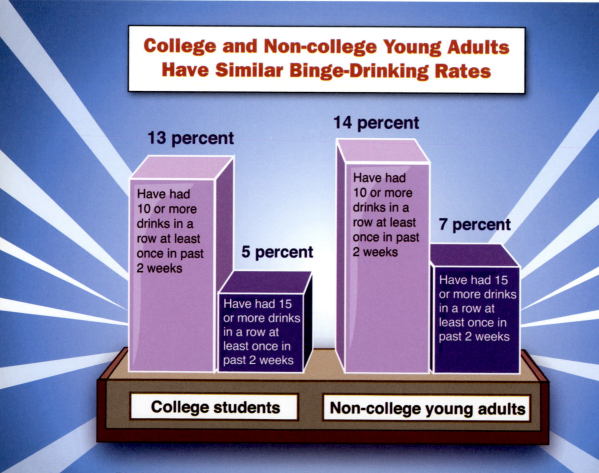

College and Non-college Young Adults Have Similar Binge-Drinking Rates

13 percent — Have had 10 or more drinks in a row at least once in past 2 weeks

5 percent — Have had 15 or more drinks in a row at least once in past 2 weeks

14 percent — Have had 10 or more drinks in a row at least once in past 2 weeks

7 percent — Have had 15 or more drinks in a row at least once in past 2 weeks

College students

Non-college young adults

Taken from: Lloyd Johnston et al., "Volume II: College Students and Adults Ages 19–45," *Monitoring the Future: National Survey Results on Drug Use, 1975–2007*. National Institute on Drug Abuse, 2008.

crashes. In the end, alcohol kills more kids than all other drugs combined [according to the National Institute of Alcohol Abuse and Alcoholism].

Not All College Students Are Drunkards

While the statistics mentioned above are stark, and clearly indicate that alcohol misuse continues to be a problem on college campuses, it is important to recognize that there is a tremendous amount of misinformation about college drinking floating unchallenged through the media and from alcohol researchers themselves. It is also critical to recognize that lots and lots of people profit from the pervasive use of alcohol at colleges—people in the tourism industry (e.g., spring break trips), beverage manufacturers, advertisers, bar owners, grocery store chains, media outlets, and the list goes on. The same TV stations that draw in viewers with stories of alcohol-related tragedies on campuses make money from alcohol advertising. All of these factors make it very difficult to get to the truth, which is that alcohol use on college campuses is certainly a problem, but hardly the epidemic it is made out to be. . . .

There is no question that some college students drink irresponsibly and do great harm to themselves and/or others. Alcohol overdoses have claimed the lives of roughly half a dozen students since the fall of 2004. . . .

While some students push the limits of alcohol consumption and put themselves and those around them at great risk, it is unfair to assume that all college students are drunkards. The data tell a much different story—the majority of students either do not drink or do so without causing problems. However, based on media reports, it is easy to understand why so many people believe that all college students drink to excess. It is virtually impossible to read the paper or turn on the news these days without hearing ominous statistics about the supposed epidemic of alcohol abuse on college campuses. . . .

Media Make Us Think College Drinking Is Rampant

Last year [2008], one of my students told me an interesting story about her spring break experience in Jamaica. She said that she walked out onto a sparsely populated beach and noticed a small group of people crammed into a small area of sand, with TV cameras focused on them. It was MTV and they were clearly trying to capture footage that American consumers want to see—kids going crazy on their wild spring break trip to Jamaica. Few advertisers would pay to push their products in between footage of an empty beach in Jamaica, so they were apparently trying to create the illusion of craziness as best they could. This is certainly not to suggest that spring break trips are zen-like experiences for most students—the point is often to go to some far off place and get drunk repeatedly over a period of a week. However, the public do not see episodes of MTV Spring Break in which students volunteer to build homes for the homeless, deliver food aid in foreign countries, etc, they simply see craziness, even if it has to be manufactured by the media to give the public what they want. A little digging quickly turns up plenty of alternatives to stereotypical spring break trips.

Have you ever seen a movie about college life in which heavy drinking was not a central theme? I haven't. If you ask college students how much they think other students drink, the numbers that they provide are often way beyond the reality of the situation. For some reason, we as a society have convinced ourselves that drinking on college campuses has reached an unheard of level and that the situation is quite dire. Is this true? Let's take a look at the data.

According to Henry Wechsler and colleagues at the Harvard School of Public Health, roughly 23% of students qualify as *frequent binge drinkers or frequent heavy episodic drinkers.* Binge drinking is defined as having four (females) or five (males) drinks during a single evening, and frequent binge drinking means doing this three or more times during a two week period. Frequent binge drinkers consume roughly 68% of all of the alcohol on college campuses and do most of the damage, including the damage to the reputations of college students as a whole.

It Is All About Media "Spin"

Dr. Wechsler's data suggest that the number of students that fall into the frequent binge drinking category has increased significantly during the past decade, from roughly 20% to 23%. However, it is almost always overlooked that the number of students that abstain from drinking has also increased significantly, 16% to 19%. As a result, the data could be spun in two different ways—either raising alarm by suggesting that an epidemic is brewing or praising the growing number of abstainers for making healthy choices. Indeed, if one looks at the magnitude of shift in drinking habits, the proportionate change in abstention rates outpaced the rise in heavy drinking rates. Clearly, the media have chosen to focus on the increase in heavy episodic drinking and the public have responded with both concern and great interest. The concern and interest combine to increase viewership, which helps media outlets sell advertising. The cycle then simply continues to feed on itself. I am well aware of this fact, having had my own research twisted by reporters to confirm the myth that college drinking is completely out of control.

On a side note, one ironic and unfortunate aspect of this entire process is that, during the same commercial break in which a reporter might foreshadow an evening news report about the dangers of college drinking, one might see several commercials for alcoholic beverages. Scary news about drinking draws viewers close while beer commercials attempt to sell them the same product that they are supposed to be worried about!

The public should be aware that researchers have essentially no control over how the media spin their research findings. In the end, simply because a reporter refers to a published study does not mean that they are accurately reporting on the outcomes or the implications.

The truth about college drinking is far more complicated than it is made out to be in the media. Alcohol misuse on American college campuses is certainly a problem, in some ways a big problem, and we need to find a way to deal with it. The number of students suffering from alcohol misuse, their own or someone else's, has increased over the years, and Emergency Room visits seem to be on the rise. However, such data *do not* necessarily indicate that there is a true epidemic of alcohol abuse at colleges across the country. The majority of the alcohol-related problems seem to be caused by a minority of students. Not all college drinkers get out of hand, drink to get drunk, require treatment for alcohol poisoning, etc. Indeed, if one looks at trend data from nationwide surveys that assess college alcohol use, levels of alcohol use, even levels of heavy episodic alcohol use (e.g., 5+ drinks per occasion at least once in a two week period), have either remained relatively stable or decreased in the past 20 years. . . .

Looking More Closely at Binge-Drinking Data

As indicated above, the number of alcohol-related consequences on college campuses has apparently been on the rise. Several universities, including Harvard have reported increases in the number of students arriving at Emergency Rooms for alcohol poisoning. How can this be if the percentage of students that binge-drink has remained relatively stable? Wechsler and colleagues suggest that the rise in consequences is directly tied to an increase in the number of *frequent* binge drinkers (i.e., three or more binges . . . in two week period). On the surface, this hypothesis seems to make sense, and is backed up by data showing a relationship between frequency of binge drinking and likelihood of suffer-

ing consequences. Frequency of binge drinking could certainly increase the chances of getting in arguments or fights, being a victim of sexual assault, being injured in accidents, etc. However, there doesn't seem to be any logical reason why binge drinking often would, by itself, increase the odds of suffering an overdose requiring medical assistance. If four or five drinks doesn't cause a person to overdose and die during a single night (which it shouldn't), then why would drinking at that threshold three or more times per two week period increase your risk of such consequences?

The binge-drinking threshold for women is having four drinks in quick succession; for men, it is five. (© Chris Rout/Alamy)

The most logical explanation is really quite simple. Binge drinking is a threshold. Those that have the requisite number of drinks are classified as binge drinkers while those that fall under the threshold are classified as non-binge drinkers. The percentage of students that are binge drinkers has remained relatively unchanged. *However*, sorting students into just two categories tells us virtually nothing about how heavily the students actually drink. A female student would qualify as a binge drinker if she had four drinks or forty drinks. Thus, it is entirely possible that peak levels of consumption beyond the binge threshold have been skyrocketing over the years, and we have simply missed this fact because of the focus on binge vs. non-binge drinking.

By analogy, according to CDC [Centers for Disease Control and Prevention] data regarding how much Americans weigh, the percentage of Americans meeting the criteria for being overweight increased from roughly 45% to 65% between 1960–2000. That represents roughly a 50% increase [in] the number of people that are overweight. At the same time, obesity increased from 13% to 31%, a change of roughly 250%! Just looking at the number of people that surpass the overweight threshold tells us little about how far beyond the threshold they actually go. It is quite possible that a similar situation has occurred with drinking levels on college campuses.

College Students Are Not the Only Ones Who Drink

Obviously, college students are not the only people on the planet that occasionally drink more than they should. However, compared to their non-college peers, they do tend to drink more heavily. Interestingly, if one looks at the drinking levels of high school students, those bound for college tend to drink less while in high school, but then quickly begin to out-drink their non-college peers once arriving at college. Alcohol use then tapers off again once college students graduate. In other words, there really seems to be something about the college environment that promotes, or at least supports, higher than normal levels of alcohol consumption. . . .

It is important to point out that heavy drinking college students do not represent a random slice of the college demographic. Some students are much more likely than others to drink irresponsibly. The prototypical hard drinking college student is a Caucasian male fraternity member at a homogeneous institution with a high density of alcohol outlets and cheap drink prices. As a group, these individuals drink more heavily than other students. African-American students drink the least and are more likely to be abstainers than Caucasian students. Latino and Asian students typically fall somewhere in between. The type of school that a student attends plays a significant role in influencing drinking behavior. Even Caucasian male fraternity members tend to drink less when they attend schools with a large minority population. Traditionally, female students at all-female schools drink far less than females at coed institutions, though this gap is quickly closing. Indeed, females in general represent a group in which drinking levels really have been on the rise during the past few years. . . .

> **FAST FACT**
>
> According to a 2006 study in the *Journal of Studies on Alcohol*, young adults who do not attend college have a higher long-term risk of developing an alcohol-use disorder.

Many Factors Influence Student Drinking Habits

Given the high incidence of heavy drinking among Caucasian male fraternity members, it is quite tempting to conclude that the fraternity environment produces students that drink heavily. This might be partially true, but there is now clear evidence that the fraternity environment is not completely to blame. We have observed, as have others, that students who drink heavily during high school are more likely to join fraternities at college and continue to drink heavily. In other words, it appears that many students join fraternities in part because their existing tendency to drink heavily is embraced.

We have also observed that drinking habits tend to shift as students progress through their college careers. Specifically, freshmen tend to drink less often than seniors, but they drink much more heavily when they do drink. Because drinking is illegal for the vast majority of freshmen, it appears that they drink opportunistically, consuming the alcohol that they have quickly so that they will have a buzz when they go out to parties or bars where they might not have access to more alcohol. People in the college health field often refer to this as *frontloading.*

There are several other variables that influence the drinking habits of students. For instance, students who attend schools with a high density of alcohol outlets, particularly those offering cheap drinks, are more likely to drink heavily than those at schools where alcohol policies are strictly enforced and access to alcohol is limited.

The take home message here should be fairly obvious —while some college students do drink irresponsibly, not all students do, and those that do drink irresponsibly *do not* represent a random sample of all college students.

Alcoholics Anonymous and Other 12-Step Programs Are Effective

Judith Eaton

In the following viewpoint Judith Eaton asserts that Alcoholics Anonymous (AA) is an effective treatment program that helps those struggling with alcohol and substance abuse achieve sobriety. Eaton tells her own personal story about how AA enabled her to beat her addiction to alcohol and prescription drugs. She says that AA helps people struggling with addictions do more than just abstain from their addiction. It helps them to abstain and move to an enlightened spiritual and emotional state. Eaton believes that spirituality is important to an addict's quest to quit. Willpower alone is not enough, she says. AA works, says the author, because it is a spiritual program. Eaton is a psychiatrist in Worcester, Massachusetts.

A s one of the anonymous writers (a doctor) of the 3rd edition of the book *Alcoholics Anonymous* said, "What is this power that AA possesses? This creative power? I don't know what it is. I suppose the doctor

SOURCE: Judith Eaton, "Medicine, Spirituality, and Alcoholics Anonymous: A Personal Story," *Southern Medical Journal*, v. 100, April 2007. Reproduced by permission.

might say, 'This is psychosomatic medicine.' I suppose the psychiatrist might say, 'This is benevolent interpersonal relations.' I suppose others would say 'This is a group psychotherapy.' To me, it is God."

The Power of the Group

However, for me, the specific power of AA is the fellowship itself. I trust it completely. AA is a group of people, once miserable and desperate, now happy and grateful in recovery. It is a group that is totally disparate in its makeup, with people from all walks of life and with differing histories—yet we all have the same basic story and the same feelings. It is a group that knows it can hold on to the gift of sobriety only if it gives it away to other alcoholics who still suffer. There are no leaders, just the power of the group. It is a group of people who will accept all comers. As is stated in the preamble of AA, "The only requirement for membership is a desire to stop drinking."

My own early experience with God was being raised in the Roman Catholic Church. I learned all I had to know by memorizing the catechism and doing all the rituals. I actually liked all that; I never had to think about ethics or morality. It was all spelled out. I did not have to make decisions about sexuality or how to treat people. There were rules for all this. I was even a bit of a fanatic, going to great lengths to find ways to attend Mass while on call as a pediatric resident. I loved the Mass in Latin and the rituals. I liked not connecting with other people and just being submersed in this special club. I believed exactly everything I was told. According to Chet Raymo, a physicist, "Religion in particular provides a sense of belonging to a group, a history, a culture in which to take pride, great works of art, stirring literature, service to the poor and needy, satisfying liturgical celebrations and rites of passage. It provides the consolation of belonging to the one true faith, of being an insider."

The author says that Alcoholics Anonymous helps alcoholics achieve sobriety by supporting changes in its members' spiritual and emotional states. (Larry Mulvehill/Photo Researchers, Inc.)

However, my religion and that of many others seemed to be focused on keeping oneself out of eternal damnation by following rules. AA, by contrast, is focused on not drinking and on helping others to attain sobriety. "Sobriety" is a change in a person's spiritual and emotional state, which accompanies not drinking. "Abstinence" is just not drinking. AA is about sobriety.

Trying to Quit on My Own

Back in my own drinking days, depression escalated with my substance use. Therefore, my early attempts at sobriety involved having myself admitted to a mental hospital and, later, to a long-term treatment facility. I believed that I drank because I was depressed; that I was not an alcoholic. If only my depression would lift, I would not need to drink so much any more, or to take drugs.

My religion at this point just seemed to disappear. There was no epiphany or dramatic loss of faith. It just sort of petered out and I never felt its loss. It was not a sense of being let down by God or of being angry at Him. He was just not in the picture any longer. I was admitted to a therapeutic community and stayed for two years. This experience introduced me to the idea of people helping one another directly without the intermediary of clergy or professional helpers. It was also the first time I felt at home, despite wide differences in the backgrounds of my fellow addicts in treatment. I thought that I emerged from the therapeutic community "cured" and not needing any follow-up or 12-step program. In fact, we ridiculed AA. Also, since this particular therapeutic community was for drug addicts, many of us thought that we could still drink in safety. After all, wasn't alcoholism a different problem altogether? Unfortunately, I found that this was not true.

For the next 18 years, I managed to stay out of major trouble with just occasional misuse of prescription medications. My drugs of choice were amphetamines, barbiturates and tranquilizers—and alcohol, of course. I finally came to the realization that my drinking was not compatible with the clean and sober life I thought I was living and I stopped drinking. I remained abstinent (not drinking) for the next 2 years, but I was still occasionally misusing prescription medications. I convinced myself that these were necessary. Looking back, I still had not found the psychological and spiritual aspects of recovery. I was not involved with AA or any other fellowship. I was alone in my abstinence, which I attributed to my own superior willpower.

I finally decided to go to an AA meeting and once again felt that sense of being home, no longer alone, and safe. I honestly do not know why I began to go after all this time. Some of my AA friends would say it was "by the Grace of God," but I hold staunchly to my unbelief and will never admit that. In any case, I began to work the AA program: "Don't drink, go to meetings, ask for help," and just keep doing it one day at a time for the rest of your life.

I found an AA sponsor by listening to others' stories and selecting someone who had worked on some similar issues to my own. A sponsor is someone who has experienced the pain of addiction and the miracle of recovery, who can serve as a guide for working the 12 steps, and who can provide suggestions and advice for working through other aspects of the AA program. She is not a therapist or an instructor. My sponsor was willing to let me find my own higher power and did not insist that I accept "God." She shared her own struggles as well as successes. I learned that in AA we help each other. This is quite different from psychotherapy when one person is the identified patient and the other is the identified well person.

Working a 12-Step Program Is Simple *and* Difficult

Working a 12-step program is both very simple and very difficult. There is no specific time frame for working the steps and there is no endpoint. There are no grades and no graduation, just a better sense of self and self-esteem. There is no single correct way to work through these steps. I was worried initially that I could not work the steps because I did not believe in a personal God, but I found a way that worked for me.

Step One

We admitted we were powerless over alcohol—that our lives had become unmanageable. This is the step of surrender, which was an easy step for me to accept. I knew I was powerless over even one drink. I was powerless to talk myself out of rationalizations for taking pills. I had made promises to myself over and over to stop or control my use and I had broken them all. I finally realized I could not control my substance use on my own.

Step Two

Came to believe that a Power greater than ourselves could restore us to sanity. Having realized my own powerlessness, it was necessary for me to find a power greater that myself that could help me stay sober. It was a great relief to give up the struggle for control, the endless pursuit of will power strong enough to make things work right. I felt I no longer had to try to fix or "cure" myself. My way was not working and I had to find another possible solution.

This step seems counterintuitive to some people at first because we have tried so hard for so long to muster up the willpower to control our use. Willpower can work in the short run, but sooner or later the urge to drink becomes overwhelming. If willpower then is the answer, we need to surrender the struggle.

As a psychiatrist, I took issue with the step 2 notion of "insanity" because that meant florid psychosis to me. However, the definition offered by AA is that insanity is doing the same thing over and over again and expecting different results. I had tried so many times to control my drinking and ultimately had failed, which clearly made me eligible for the AA definition of "insanity."

Step Three

Made a decision to turn our will and our lives over to the care of God as we understood Him. This was a major stumbling block for me because I did not believe in a personal God, nor do I now. The important operative words in step 3 are "as we understood him." For me, there is a very powerful force in AA, a spiritual force that I do not choose to call "God." It is the truthfulness, the caring, the willingness to help any alcoholic at any time, the fellowship of AA itself. It is the belief that this program does work and can work for me. There is also the knowledge that I cannot do it alone, without the "higher power" of the AA fellowship.

Step Four

Made a searching and fearless moral inventory of ourselves. This step required me to take a critical look at how I had run my life and how it affected others. There are different ways to accomplish step 4. I wrote down a history of my substance use, including resentments and feelings I had against others while I was drinking. I did not do this to look for causes or blame, but rather to look at my own responsibility for each and every negative event and reaction. Through the course of my drinking and drug use, I became very good at finding ways to blame others for almost everything. Now I had to take a long hard look at myself, and I also had to take responsibility for my own behavior: Just because I have the illness of alcoholism, this does not give me an excuse to behave badly.

Step Five

Admitted to God, to ourselves and to another human being the exact nature of our wrongs. I choose to do this step with my sponsor. Other people may choose a clergy person or a therapist. I sat down with my sponsor and read to her my fearless moral inventory written down as part of step 4. Since I had been in psychotherapy off and on for years, this was not a new concept for me. However, the purpose of step 5 is different from that of therapy or confession, in that I simply told my sponsor the story of my addiction. I was not seeking forgiveness or treatment. Step 5 teaches us not to keep secrets. It was a relief to tell my sponsor about my past, and to have her respond with some of her own struggles from her own personal history.

Step Six

We are entirely ready to have God remove all these defects of character. After taking a good hard look at myself and sharing it with my sponsor, I began to realize I had defects of character that I needed to have removed. Having had lifelong depression, I certainly had a list of things I hated about myself. However, character defects differ in that they could be changed with the help of a higher power. Some of my defects had even seemed like assets; for example, the ability to work constantly. Paradoxically, it seems, I had to be willing to give up even those defects that I rather liked.

Step Seven

Humbly asked Him to remove our shortcomings. For some people this step involves praying to God. For me it is a continuing mindfulness of what I need to change, and a willingness to try to improve myself by growing in the AA program. It also helped to have a sponsor who was willing to point out my character defects from time to time, and explain how they can threaten my sobriety.

Step Eight

Made a list of all persons we had harmed, and became willing to make amends to them all. This step is done as another follow-up to the "fearless, moral inventory" of step 4. I remembered and listed to the best of my ability the people who had been harmed by my past behavior. This was harder than it sounds. I was often impaired in one way or another, and did not realize at the time the effect my actions had on others. There was also the harm done to nameless people in my life, like letting them down when I was drunk by not showing up for important events in their lives.

The second part of step 8 required me to become willing to make amends. This was difficult to do, especially in those instances that involved people who had also harmed me. However, it was a very necessary part of the recovery process. It is through making amends for past wrongs to others that we regain our self respect.

Step Nine

Made direct amends to such people whenever possible, except when to do so would injure them or others. In this step I actually connected with the people I had harmed and made amends. For some people this could mean repaying stolen funds, etc, but for me it was less concrete. I needed to offer apologies, while being mindful that I should not try to manipulate the person's response, a skill at which I was very proficient. I learned that one does not work step 9 to gain forgiveness, but simply because it is necessary to grow spiritually and emotionally.

FAST FACT

In 2006, 4 million persons aged twelve or older (1.6 percent of the population) received some kind of treatment for a problem related to the use of alcohol or illicit drugs, according to the National Survey on Drug Use and Health.

Step Ten

Continued to take personal inventory and when we were wrong promptly admitted it. This step means to me that I do not have to become perfect. I may continue to behave in a manner that is stupid or hurtful at times, but I need to be aware of that and make amends as soon as possible. It is dangerous for me to expect perfection because it negates my humanness, which was what I previously tried to eliminate with alcohol and drugs. AA emphasizes "progress, not perfection."

Step Eleven

Sought through prayer and meditation to improve our conscious contact with God, as we understood Him, praying only for knowledge of His will for us and the power to carry that out. This step requires me to be conscious of a Higher Power and a higher purpose in my life. I try to stop and listen to myself and others, so that I can learn what the next right thing to do is. I try to lead a life full of worthy actions so as to have a feeling of positive self esteem.

Step Twelve

Having had a spiritual awakening as the result of these steps, we tried to carry this message to alcoholics and to practice these principles in all our affairs. Each person in AA defines "spiritual awakening" in his/her own way. For me, it is the awareness that through the fellowship of AA I have become a better person. I have been given the gift of a better life, and I try to share the AA way of life with anyone who might want it. I do some of this professionally, when I work with other physicians affected by substance abuse. I try to live my life in such a way that it can be a power of example to doctors who cannot imagine themselves ever attending an AA meeting.

I am also available to help other alcoholics, by simply taking them to an AA meeting, or by sharing with them my own experience, strength and hope. This is what keeps me sober. It is one of the most powerful principles of AA—that each one of us is always responsible whenever an alcoholic asks for help. We can do this by as simple an act as making coffee at an AA meeting or by a more dramatic act such as taking someone to a hospital for treatment.

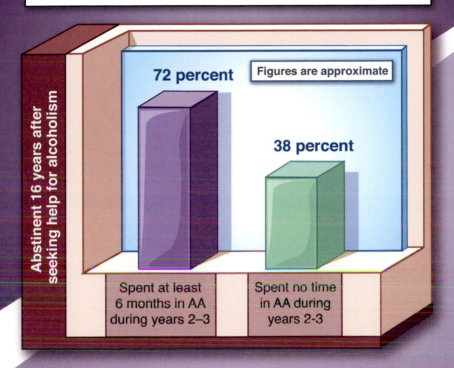

Attending Alcoholics Anonymous (AA) Helps People Stay Abstinent

Abstinent 16 years after seeking help for alcoholism

72 percent

Figures are approximate

38 percent

| Spent at least 6 months in AA during years 2–3 | Spent no time in AA during years 2-3 |

Taken from: Rudolf and Bernice Moos, "Participation in Treatment and Alcoholics Anonymous: A 16-year Follow-up of Initially Untreated Individuals," *Journal of Clinical Psychology*, June 2006.

AA Works

Sometimes I sit in an AA meeting and just marvel at the process. Here is a group of wounded people willing to be open and honest with one another, to help ourselves and everyone else in the room. We often do not know each others' last names, nor do we know what others do for a living. We may not have ever met the other person before. However, we all know feelings—good and bad—and we believe that the power in the room will be there and help us stay sober. That it is worth the pain and risk of sharing ourselves.

As a physician, I have from time to time pondered what makes the program work. I don't let myself think about that too long because the analysis does not help. AA works because it is a spiritual program relying on a Higher Power to keep people from succumbing to the chronic, fatal illness of alcoholism. We do the work that leads to spiritual change and growth. We give it away to others to keep the gift of recovery.

Alcoholics Anonymous and Other 12-Step Programs Are Not Effective

Melanie Solomon

In the following viewpoint Melanie Solomon contends that Alcoholics Anonymous (AA) and other 12-step programs are not that effective. According to Solomon, statistics show that AA only works for about 5 percent of people. Unfortunately, says Solomon, the vast majority of treatment programs are based on AA's principles, and most people believe that 12-step programs are the only way to achieve sobriety. According to Solomon, this is out-of-date thinking. Scientifically based research has provided alternatives to AA programs. According to Solomon, many people even achieve recovery from their addiction without the help of any form of treatment program. She implores people struggling with alcohol addiction to look beyond AA. Solomon is the author of *AA—Not the Only Way; Your One Stop Resource Guide to 12-Step Alternatives.*

"Keep coming back, it works if you work it!" This is what is chanted at the end of every meeting, but what if you *have* "worked it" and you still keep going back and getting drunk or loaded?

Now, most people in the program will say things like, "Well, you must not have really done the steps right," or "You didn't go to *enough* meetings," or "You didn't pray to your Higher Power," or "You know you did *something wrong* or else you would still be sober!"

Since what you are told from your very first 12-step meeting is, "Your only options are to get sober using our Program, or it's jails, institutions or death," you tend to stop thinking for yourself, (since it was your "best thinking that got you here"), stop questioning, and just follow what others tell you to do.

AA Hardly a Proven Method

This would be fine if this is what worked . . . but unfortunately, evidence is proving otherwise.

The 12-step success rate is showing to be approximately 3 percent [according to Gerald Brown, co-founder of the Baldwin Research Institute]. Yes, that's right . . . only 3 percent! Here are some more startling statistics:

- 45% of the people who attend Alcoholics Anonymous (AA) meetings never return after their first meeting.
- 95% never return after the first year.
- 5% retention rate (Based on Alcoholics Anonymous World Services' own statistics).
- 93–97% of conventional drug rehabs and alcohol treatment centers are 12-step or AA based, so those who leave AA to look elsewhere, such as conventional alcohol and drug treatment for solutions, are essentially rejoining AA!

AA hardly sounds like a "proven method," let alone one that works for most people. So, if only about 5% of

the people are getting the help that they need, what about the 95% of the people who are not being helped? That is the purpose of this article . . . to provide much needed awareness to individuals, rehabilitation centers, hospitals, sober livings, and even 12-step programs themselves so that people with substance abuse problems can be helped.

The bottom line is this . . . is the goal to get alcoholics and addicts into AA or NA [Narcotics Anonymous] or CA [Cocaine Anonymous] or is it to actually get them help?

The author contends that, since the success rate of Alcoholics Anonymous is only 3 percent, the program is ultimately unsuccessful. (Larry Mulvehill/Photo Researchers, Inc.)

Addiction Is Not a "One-Size-Fits-All" Problem

Let me mention from the start that I think 12-step programs are wonderful for those individuals who it does work for. I have seen it change many lives for the better, including my dad, who has now had 15 years of continuous sobriety, maintaining his sobriety from his very first meeting.

It is also a great fellowship to share experiences, strength and hope. So, in no way am I anti-AA.

However, it is becoming clearer to me that substance abuse is not a "one-size-fits-all" problem, and therefore, there can not be a "one-size-fits-all" solution.

The National Institute of Drug Abuse, NIDA, has even gone on record to emphasize that no single addiction treatment method is right for everyone. They claim that matching treatment services to each individual's specific needs is critical to success.

In addition, research studies indicate that even the most severely addicted individuals can participate actively in their own treatment, and that active participation is essential for good outcomes. According to the NIDA, counseling, either individual or group, and other behavioral therapies are critical components of effective treatment for addiction.

AA Is Not the Only Way

It's interesting to note that participation in a 12-step program was never mentioned anywhere in this research based guide which discussed the principles of effective treatment.

Reliance on outdated and ineffective treatment methods has created an environment that fully expects individuals to fail, and fail again until such time that rock bottom has been reached.

It is often said that once an individual has reached rock bottom that there is only one way to go, *up*. The problem with that philosophy is that for many people, the ultimate rock bottom is death [says Lloyd Vacovsky, executive director of the American Council on Alcoholism].

Vacovsky goes on to write:

> Many, (if not indeed most) alcohol dependent individuals have lost faith in themselves, and more importantly hope for the future. It is common for such individuals to have numerous attempts at sobriety, most often using 12-step methods. They have been programmed to accept themselves as hopeless and powerless, with their chance for recovery being slim to none. . . . It is up to the individual to determine what the most appropriate treatment is. It is up to the treatment community to provide options that set up individuals to succeed, rather than be expected to fail.

Sadly, Americans are largely unaware that such options even exist. At least, the general public is. While the public is being told that "turning your will and life over to the care of God as you understand Him," as AA suggests, is the only treatment for their illness, scientifically based research has been going on for decades. Results of this research are threefold:

1. We now have options for treatment that are based on science rather than fundamentalist religion;
2. Gives back choice and a sense of control to the individual, which is proving to be extremely important and
3. We now have evidence that is in direct contradiction to the traditional view of problem drinking.

Research Suggests That AA's Principles May Be Wrong

What, exactly, is the research finding? Here is what some of the experts in the addiction field . . . have found:

- Well-designed research conducted over more than three decades has conclusively demonstrated that problem drinking will not inevitably get progressively worse, and that this is one attribute of being a "disease" of alcoholism is simply wrong. Some problem drinkers "progress," but the vast majority don't.
- What most Americans believe about drinking problems and their treatment is substantially inaccurate.
- Drinking problems do not occur as a result of a disease. It is a learned behavior, and additional learning can therefore modify behavior.
- For no other "disease" do so many physicians, psychologists and counselors themselves believe in the non-research-based myths of problem drinking, ignoring the research of their own peers in developing their treatment plans.
- "Problem drinkers in the United States are faced with a daunting dilemma when they seek help. They can either accept the prevailing myth that abstinence is the only effective means to resolve a drinking problem, or they can be accused of being "in denial. . . ."
- Insistence by treatment programs to only offer abstinence has been shown to deter many problem drinkers from seeking treatment.
- Individualizing treatment is crucial.
- Chronic "relapsers" can actually be harmed by the 12-step model view that once a slip has started, you are powerless to stop; the stronger one's belief in this is the longer and more damaging the relapses are.
- The confrontation and treating alcoholics and addicts like children commonly thought necessary to help them actually often hinders any change.
- Many providers deliberately resist change because they have too much of an attachment to their own

ideas of what should work, claiming, "I know what worked for me, and I'm sure that it can work for everyone else as long as they just do what I say."

- The only way to resolve a problem with alcohol is to abstain for life is wrong for the majority of people. A substantial proportion becomes moderate drinkers even when achieving abstinence is the primary focus of treatment.
- Dr. Patricia Owen, Director of Research of the Hazelden Foundation, who was a long-time supporter of abstinence-only treatment, referred to these individuals as "in recovery without abstinence" and acknowledged their presence in large numbers among a sample of Hazelden graduates.

Of course, not even all scientists agree on the nature of and best treatments for alcohol abuse. But this is the twenty-first century, and no one would disagree that all patients suffering with an alcohol or drug problem have a right, just like any other patient suffering with any other problem, to be fully informed of the available options, the risks or areas of uncertainty, and, after reviewing the relevant information, in consultation with one or more providers, choose a course of action.

This is simply good, ethical medicine. Should people struggling with substance abuse issues accept anything less?

Treatment Programs Are Not Always Necessary

It is also important to acknowledge that recovery programs are not necessary to discover how to quit and stay quit.

The following is from the Harvard Medical School's *Mental Health Letter*, the August/September 1996 issue:

> Most recovery from alcoholism is not the result of treatment. Only 20% of alcohol abusers are ever treated. . . . Alcohol addicts, like heroin addicts, have a tendency to mature out of their addiction. . . .

Most People Classified as Needing Alcohol or Substance Abuse Treatment Do Not Think They Need It

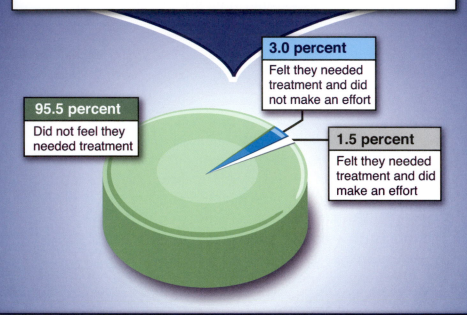

3.0 percent
Felt they needed treatment and did not make an effort

95.5 percent
Did not feel they needed treatment

1.5 percent
Felt they needed treatment and did make an effort

There are 21.1 million people who need, but are not receiving, treatment for illicit drug or alcohol use.

Taken from: 2006 National Survey on Drug Use and Health, U.S. Substance Abuse and Mental Health Services Administration.

In a group of self-treated alcoholics, more than half said that they had simply thought it over and decided that alcohol was bad for them. Another group said health problems and frightening experiences such as accidents and blackouts persuaded them to quit. . . .

Others have recovered by changing their circumstances with the help of a new job or a new love or under the threat of a legal crisis or the breakup of a family.

Study results from addiction researchers, Doctors Linda and Mark Sobell, confirm Harvard's 20% treatment statistic:

Surveys found that over 77 percent of those who had overcome an alcohol problem had done so without treatment. In an earlier study . . . a sizable majority of alcohol abusers, 82 percent, recovered on their own.

However, even though it is possible to recover on your own, you may want a recovery program, or at least a licensed professional for support.

Time to Stop Living in the Dark Ages of Recovery

The good news is that many more treatment programs are starting to provide more evidence-based options beyond just the traditional 12-step approach, and this list is growing everyday.

It is finally time to stop living in the dark ages of recovery, educate people about all of their choices and alternatives that are out there and maybe start making a dent in the alcohol and drug use problem that millions are facing each day instead of continuing to perpetuate it.

If you are one of those people who still believe that the 12-steps are the "only way" to recover, I implore you to have an open mind.

In fact, Bill W., one of the co-founders of AA said, "It would be a product of false pride to claim that A.A. is a cure-all, even for alcoholism." Bill W. repeatedly said that "our hats are off to you if you can find a better way" and "If [those seeking a different cure] can do better by other means, we are glad."

CHAPTER 3

Personal Stories About Alcoholism

A Firefighter's Struggle with Alcoholism

Wendy Harris

In the following article Wendy Harris tells the story of former firefighter Jon Sustachek and how alcohol permeated his life. Sustachek awakens one morning, a sick and withered man who can barely hold a glass of water to his lips. He calls 911, and the realization of what forty years of heavy drinking have done to him finally sets in. Harris recounts how Sustachek began drinking as a young boy with his father and how as a fireman he and his buddies always found a reason to drink. According to Harris, Sustachek is not an anomaly in the state of Wisconsin. For many Wisconsinites, especially those of German or eastern European heritage, drinking is a way of life. Harris tells Sustachek's story and also discusses Wisconsin's alcohol heritage. Jon Sustachek's realization of how alcohol has destroyed his health is one of several stories written by journalist Wendy Harris for a 2008 exposé on alcohol's impact on the state of Wisconsin in the *Appleton (WI) Post Crescent*. Other stories recount how Sustachek finds out that he needs a new liver, how he gets that new liver, and how it gives him a second chance at life.

He woke up tired, foggy-headed and wickedly thirsty. This hangover was unlike any other. Maybe it was the flu, he thought.

Jon Sustachek shuffled down the hall on skinny legs that wobbled under the weight of his bloated belly and stopped in the bathroom.

SOURCE: Wendy Harris, "The Redemption of Jon Sustachek," *Appleton Post-Crescent*, July 12, 2008. Reproduced by permission.

Photo on facing page. One-on-one counseling has proved to be effective in helping alcoholics recover from their addiction. (John Greim/Photo Researchers, Inc.)

In the mirror was a man with yellow eyes and skin the color of a pumpkin, a man with a ruined liver, a dying man.

But Jon didn't notice.

Denial played its part. But, more than that, alcohol had numbed his senses and dulled his awareness. Was it morning or night?

Leaving the bathroom for the kitchen, he picked up a glass with trembling hands and held it under the tap. But as he raised the glass, his hand shook so hard the water sloshed out, never reaching his lips.

This was what it had come to. Jon, the alcoholic son of a father who had died prematurely of a heart attack, was close to claiming his heritage in full. In a moment of lucidity, he knew he was in trouble.

But there was no one to help him; he was alone, having driven away his family with his drinking. His ex-wife and their oldest daughter, now an adult, lived together a couple miles away, but he did not call them or even think of doing so. Nor did he call his youngest daughter, a nurse who lived across town.

Jon reached for the phone on the wall and called 911. Then he made his way across the living room and lowered himself into a tan recliner.

There, as he sat in his favorite chair in front of a window looking out on the dark of a winter's night, Jon's life of 61 years pooled around him.

Four decades of heavy drinking had caught up with him. Drinking with fellow firefighters in dim smoky bars. Drinking at home alone in the basement. Drinking that covered his liver with knobby scars. Drinking that laid the foundation for some relationships while wrecking others.

Drinking that had brought him, finally, on this snow-encrusted December night in 2005, to a moment of reckoning.

Wisconsin's Drinking Legacy

There is an unparalleled culture of drinking in Wisconsin, and it is woven inextricably through the fabric of life.

A great many Wisconsinites, true to our heritage, either German or Eastern European, find no shortage of excuses to imbibe. We drink at bars, church functions, charity events, community festivals and even youth-league baseball games.

Wisconsin's drinking culture at once benefits the state handsomely and costs it dearly.

Economically, alcohol is a boon to Wisconsin. The state's 3,000 drinking establishments, employing some 14,000 people, ring up more than $600 million annually. And, in 2006, the brewing industry had a $3.35 billion impact on the state's economy, including jobs for some 30,000 residents.

But, on the other side of the ledger, drinking exacts a high toll. In 2005, at least 590 people died in Wisconsin as a direct result of alcohol use or abuse. Another 5,992 people were injured that year and some 80,000 people were arrested as a result of alcohol use or abuse, according to a recent study on alcohol and drug use by the University of Wisconsin's Population Health Institute.

The state has the nation's highest percentage of binge drinkers, according to the U.S. Centers for Disease Control and Prevention, and averages the fifth-highest rate of alcohol dependence or abuse, the National Survey on Drug Use and Health shows.

But Wisconsinites who need treatment aren't likely to get it. The state averages the fifth-highest rate of people needing but not receiving treatment for an alcohol problem, the same survey shows.

The reasons are simple but the solutions aren't necessarily. In Wisconsin, an insurance company will pay out hundreds of thousands of dollars for an alcoholic's liver transplant but will refuse to pay for the rehabilitation that could make a transplant unnecessary.

The author says that Wisconsin is known for its culture of heavy drinking, which produces more binge drinkers than any other state. (AP Images)

Also in Wisconsin, alcoholics often aren't perceived as such because heavy drinking is likely to be seen as normal, and so they don't seek treatment.

Even in a nation where the third-leading cause of preventable death, after smoking and obesity, is alcohol abuse—it claims 85,000 lives annually in wrecks, poisonings, shootings, diseases, suicides and accidents—Wisconsin stands out.

But while many other states offset alcohol's costs with taxes, Wisconsin's beer tax, the second lowest in the nation, hasn't been raised since Lyndon B. Johnson was president.

Where alcohol is cheap and widely available and the laws governing it are lax—Wisconsin is the only state where a first drunken driving offense is considered an ordinance violation and not a crime—people drink more, social scientists and economists say.

And the more they drink, the more those around them drink.

"We have a cultural myth in this country that everything a person does is self-determined and it's an individual decision," says Richard Yoast, the American Medical Association's expert on alcohol abuse and founder of Wisconsin's Clearinghouse and Prevention Resource Center on Alcohol and Other Drugs.

"The reality is that we are all very responsive to our environment. . . . If people around you are drinking (heavily), then that is what you think is normal."

For every alcoholic, the lives of [at] least four other people are directly affected, according to Al-Anon, an international support group for families and friends of alcoholics.

So it was with Jon Sustachek, who sat drinking night after night, year after year with fellow firefighters in Racine. His is the story of Wisconsin's drinking culture, his bathroom mirror a window on its potential effects, his orange face the face of a cautionary tale.

Jon, now 64, is a casualty of the drinking culture, but he also may be counted among its facilitators. He and his friends at once enabled and were influenced by each other's drinking.

That intricate, sprawling web and the things that can get tangled up and die in it—marriages, dreams, dignity, hope and love—aren't reflected in any dataset.

They're reflected in people like Jon, whose journey is about struggle and pain, reconciliation and finding hope when it seems utterly lost.

Addiction Starts Young

Born on a hot July day in 1944, Jon grew up in a middle-class family in a blue-collar town proud of its innovators and industries.

Following World War II, Racine enjoyed an economic boom, with good paying jobs for anyone lacking education but willing to work hard.

Industrial giants including S.C. Johnson—maker of Windex, Saran Wrap and Spray 'n Wash, to name a few—and heavy equipment manufacturer J.I. Case imbued Racine's growing middle class with the American dream: a cozy three-bedroom, one-bathroom house on a tree-lined street, a new car and summer vacations to Door County or beyond.

Company executives, meanwhile, built mansions along Racine's lakeshore, a few even inspired by Frank Lloyd Wright. The famous architect designed the Johnson Wax Administration Building, which remains in use today. Tourists and Wright devotees flock to the site to admire the sweeping curves of the 14-story tower, which rises from a sprawling, artistic display of Cherokee red bricks and glass tubing.

Jon's father, Harold Sustachek, built tractors at Case, hammering massive pieces of metal together in the forge shop while his mom stayed home to take care of him and his older brother and sister.

With Czechoslovakian roots, Sustacheks from a previous generation were among the first wave of Czech, Dane and German immigrants to settle in Racine.

Germans made up the majority of immigrants who came to the state, bringing their homemade beer with them.

According to the 2000 Census, German-Americans made up 42.7 percent of Wisconsin's population. Only North Dakota has a higher German-American population with 43.9 percent. (Coincidentally or not, North Dakota has the nation's second-highest rate of binge and heavy drinking.)

By the early 1900s, Racine was home to about a half-dozen breweries. Though the local breweries ultimately died out during prohibition, Racine had established itself as a drinking town. And Wisconsin was well established as a drinking state.

During Prohibition, Jon's dad learned to make beer, wine and moonshine. He did so in the basement. The hobby grew into a family affair. Harold had crocks of rotten, fermenting fruit to make wine. He had a bottle capper, too.

Jon started drinking before he was 10 years old. The parties seemed endless, the alcohol bottomless.

He enjoyed his dad's homemade beer, making sure not to drink down to the bottom of the glass so he could avoid the pulpy sediment settled there.

Jon's early imbibing was past as prologue. Drinking young is a strong predictor of abuse and addiction, research shows.

Wisconsin, on average, ranks second for the percentage of underage drinkers who use alcohol and binge drink, according to the National Survey on Drug Use and Health.

Alcohol abuse is commonly rooted in family legacies, the product of genetic predisposition and environment.

Jon's happier memories include those times spent hanging out with his father at bars. Sitting on a stool, his chin at bar level, the boy munched on potato chips that some men who drank at the bar liked to buy for him. He listened to them tell tall tales. They promised to take him on safari.

Even the family's annual summer vacation to Washington Island began in bars, Jon recalls. Starting at the Old Fashioned, they made their way up the street to the Wergland Club, across the street to the Victory Bar and then, sometimes, to Rondone's, to buy booze for the road.

They drove from bar to bar in the family Buick, with camping gear tethered to roof, inching out of Racine drink by drink. It was a slow start to a long trip; their destination, the Washington Island ferry dock was some 230 miles away.

"Being in bars was just part of our life. We didn't think anything of it," Jon recalls.

Racine is a drinker's town. A 1990 study that found Wisconsin was home to seven of the country's top 10 metropolitan areas with the most bars per capita. Racine ranked seventh behind Eau Claire, La Crosse, Kenosha, Green Bay, Milwaukee and Jersey City, N.J.

The Appleton-Oshkosh area, Scranton, Pa., and Atlantic City finished off the list, according to the study, by the National Institute on Alcohol Abuse and Alcoholism.

When Jon's dad wasn't working, he drank anything and everything. He hid his whiskey bottle in the back of the toilet to avoid incurring the wrath of his wife, Myrtle.

One bright summer day in the mid-1950s, Jon lay in bed reading a comic book. From outside his window came the electric buzz of cicadas. Then he heard another sound: his 46-year-old father crashing to the floor in the adjoining bathroom.

"I don't know how I knew, but I knew he was dead," Jon recalls.

He dropped the comic book, crawled off the bed and put on his sneakers. Slipping down the hall, he descended the stairs, bolted out the back door and ran to the nearby woods in Lincoln Field, where he cried alone.

Myrtle was now a single mom with two boys to support. She went to work at Walgreen's, earning a meager wage as a store clerk. She was chronically depressed.

Valium was her drug of choice, Jon recalls, an addiction she carried to the grave. For Jon, alcohol was a means of escape.

"When I got into high school, it was heavy, I drank to get drunk," he recalls. He drank with his buddies. He drank alone. It didn't really matter.

The stage was set. Jon's life wasn't his own anymore. It belonged to the bottle.

Alcohol, like any other drug, floods key regions of the brain with dopamine, creating a high. With repeated exposure, the brain adjusts; the availability of its own endogenous feel-good chemicals dwindles.

When the buzz is gone, the brain wants some more. The younger the brain, the more vulnerable it is to being chemically altered, explains Dr. David Friedman, a professor of physiology and pharmacology at Wake Forest University School of Medicine.

Alcohol produces a psychological dependence on par with that of cocaine, methamphetamine and opiates, Friedman says. So, while alcohol use may start with voluntary behavior, the brain eventually craves the drug as it does food or water.

One Generation to the Next

Jon was 17 when he met Sue Weber. She was 14.

Sue noticed the senior classman as he flew down the street shirtless on his Harley. He was blond, tan, handsome and muscular.

And he was always first in class to raise his hand with the answer.

"I said 'oh boy, is he ever cute,'" Sue recalls.

A friend introduced them at Racine's lakefront Fourth of July carnival. A few days later, he called and invited her to a movie.

They married a few years later in a small, traditional church wedding followed by a reception.

Sue's father arrived drunk and uninvited and fell asleep on a table. He, too, was an alcoholic whose addiction destroyed the family. Sue's brother and sister grew up to become alcoholics, with her sister dying in a car crash.

Sue was determined not to become an alcoholic. It would take her awhile to see she had married one.

Her marriage to Jon began well enough. Jon worked in a couple of factories, but, hating the grime, tedium and boredom, he was enticed by his brother-in-law's stories of being a firefighter.

Jon applied to the Racine Fire Department. They hired him when he turned 21. He fit right in. So did his drinking.

"I was an adrenaline junkie," Jon recalls. He loved the thrill of the truck company. He was one of the first to arrive on a scene for search and rescue and one of the last to leave, cleaning up after the flames turned to embers.

He played as hard as he worked, drinking more and more with his firefighter buddies.

A few years into their marriage, after giving birth to their two daughters, Monica and Jennifer, Sue grew tired of the partying. She wasn't a born drinker. She couldn't keep up with him anymore, she says.

Jon and his buddies always had a reason to drink, he recalls—Christmas parties, retirement parties, promotion parties.

His job, grueling, stressful, and often depressing, fueled his urge to drink.

FAST FACT

According to the American Liver Foundation, between 10 and 20 percent of heavy drinkers develop cirrhosis of the liver, usually after ten or more years of drinking.

"Basically, you are working in other people's misery 24 hours a day," Jon says. "Alcohol was an outlet."

At the end of a shift, Jon and other firefighters gathered at smoky corner bars and dingy taverns in the shadows of Racine's hulking factories. The bars were mostly dumps and dives, Jon recalls, but they were warm and familiar, and there was always somebody to talk to.

Firefighters are a tight-knit group, an extended family of sorts. Jon and his buddies took fishing trips up north. Jon's 14-foot fishing boat became known as the "S.S. Neversail" because it rarely made it in the water. By the time they finished at the bar, they were too drunk to fish, and it was too late anyway.

In spite of his drinking, Jon was good at his job. Search and rescue were his forte.

In a thank-you letter that hangs framed in Jon's basement bar, the Racine County sheriff wrote, "Two of your divers, namely Jon G. Sustachek and Robert M. Radewan, went to the scene and found the body of the victim within 15 minutes."

The letter is dated Dec. 29, 1976. A week earlier, the sheriff's dive team had been dispatched to frozen Tichigan Lake where a man on a snowmobile had plunged through the ice, but the team, fearing the current, wouldn't go in the water.

Jon and his partner were called to the scene and succeeded where the others hadn't.

Jon climbed the ranks of the fire department, eventually ascending to captain.

But his family life had reached a breaking point. Sue had grown weary of his drinking.

With retirement just around the corner, though, Jon's life fell apart.

On a May morning in 1997, Sue paid Jon a rare visit at the fire station.

The divorce papers were at her lawyer's office, she told him.

Their 34-year marriage was over.

"I wish I would have been stronger. I should have given him an ultimatum 20 years before that," Sue says. But she adds: "I don't think it would have helped. He never thought his drinking was a problem."

Jon retired a year and a half later.

After a few strained years, he and Sue became friends.

Looking back, he's not sure which came first, depression or even heavier drinking. But they fed off each other, at once masking and worsening his symptoms.

Without a wife or job, Jon felt no pressure to contain his drinking. He could drink whenever he wanted. He developed a routine, he recalls: Each morning, when the convenience store opened at 8, he bought a 12-pack. That got him through until the liquor store opened at 9.

After all those years of saving lives, Jon now was putting other people at risk driving drunk.

"I could have killed someone," he says. "Who knows what could have happened."

Five years ago [in 2003], a State Patrol officer pulled him over in Manitowoc County. Jon could barely walk, he recalls.

The officer handcuffed him, took him to the hospital for a blood-alcohol test and then had him locked up in jail for the night.

As the cinderblock walls closed in on Jon, he panicked. He felt claustrophobic and had panic attacks. He hyperventilated. He thought he was going to die.

"It was horrible, just horrible," he says.

"And I was so ashamed."

The downward spiral continued until after Thanksgiving 2005, when Jon holed up in his house. Through those dark winter days, he drank alone. Save for a piece of toast or maybe a half of a sandwich a day, he stopped eating, his intake limited to bottle after bottle of Ten High bourbon.

"The more I drank the more depressed I got," he says. "It was becoming a cowardly suicide."

The 911 Call

One night in December 2005, paramedics Ed Benson and Jim Dresen received a late call at Station 8.

The address, only half a mile away, was a familiar one. It's Sue's place, Benson recalls Dresen saying.

Dresen had grown up three doors down from Jon in their old Lincoln Heights neighborhood. Jon used to hang out with his older brothers.

The ambulance pulled up to the small brick and wood ranch home on Racine's north side. A foot and half of freshly fallen snow covered Jon's walkway.

Benson and Dresen knocked and waited. They knocked again. After another wait, the door finally cracked open.

There, in boxer shorts and a T-shirt, stood an old friend nearly unrecognizable to them. Could this really be the retired captain of Station 2? Just a few years earlier, they had worked alongside Jon. They had pulled broken bodies from mangled metal and burning buildings.

The Jon they knew was big and strong, with bulging calves and biceps. This man had spindly arms and legs, atrophied muscles and a large, distended belly. Like an orange pigmy, Benson thought.

Jon was incoherent, his face drawn and gaunt. He shook uncontrollably as he clung to the door.

He didn't recognize his former colleagues, men he had shared beer with at pig roasts and promotion parties.

Gently grabbing hold of him, the paramedics set him down in the recliner. They found a pair of jeans in his bedroom and his suede slippers with the lamb's wool lining.

Though it was December, Jon's calendar said it was still October.

Empty bourbon bottles lay scattered about the floor.

The paramedics loaded Jon onto the gurney and took him outside. His blood pressure was low, his pulse rapid.

Benson took Jon's hand and pressed it between his knees to keep Jon's arm still long enough to start an IV. He gave him a liter of saline and dextrose to raise his blood sugar.

They delivered Jon to All Saints Hospital in Racine.

The Orange Man

Dr. Rommell Bote had just started his shift at All Saints' emergency department.

The hospital has one of the state's busiest emergency rooms, with more than 150 patients cycling through its doors on any given day.

Bote, a master of multi-tasking, helps ease patients' anxiety with a confident smile.

As he walked across the emergency room toward the bed where Jon lay, he could see Jon was very sick.

Jon's body had been without alcohol for about 12 hours and withdrawal symptoms were hitting hard. He was sweating profusely. His heart was racing. His blood pressure was soaring. He was jaundiced, Bote recalls. He was confused and shaking.

"Right away, you could tell Jon was having manifestations of liver disease," Bote says.

Hepatic encephalopathy. Jon's liver, worn out by the ravages of alcohol, no longer could filter out toxins, so they had built up in the blood and invaded the brain, impairing cognition. It was as if Jon still were drunk.

He faded in and out of consciousness. Bote and his staff went to work to stabilize him and assess the damage.

Jon's liver was badly damaged, tests would reveal. He also was severely dehydrated, anemic and malnourished. He had pneumonia. And his blood had lost the ability to clot properly.

Jon woke up days later in the hospital's cardiac inpatient wing, covered in wires and tubes. He remembers nothing except hearing four words. Someone near his bed, he knows not who, offered him some blunt advice, straight talk that filtered through the fog into his consciousness.

"Stay dry or die."

A Son Watches His Mother Die of Alcoholism

Buddy T and D.J.

In the following story a son tells the painful tale of watching his mother die from alcohol abuse. D.J. says after he and his siblings grew older and moved out of their parents' house, his mother felt worthless and suffered from depression. Alcohol, D.J. says, soon became her best friend. D.J. describes the pain, frustration, and devastation of watching his mother drink herself to death all the while denying she had a problem. D.J. sent his story about his mother's death to Buddy T, the alcoholism guide for About.com.

There is a saying around the rooms of recovery that some alcoholics never find help "in this lifetime." In other words, they never get to the point of reaching out for help and they continue drinking all the way to the grave, all the while denying they have a problem.

For friends and family members, watching someone drink themselves to death is a lonely, frustrating and devastating experience, as D.J. describes below in this painful tale of his mother's final days.

SOURCE: Buddy T and D.J., "D.J.'s Recovery Story: 'I Am Not an Alcoholic!'" About.com, January 10, 2008. Reproduced by permission.

The viewpoint author relates his experiences in dealing with the death of his alcoholic mother. (© **Bubbles Photolibrary/Alamy**)

D.J.'s Story

On the night before Christmas there was great sorrow in my home. My mother passed away at the age of 60. She didn't have cancer. No heart attack. She didn't get in a bad car accident nor was she shot. There were no heroics that put her in harm's way nor was there someone else's wrong-doing that brought her to her demise.

In her eyes, her life became of less value as she grew older. Her children moved away and she didn't see her grandchildren as much as she had liked. She did have a loving husband, but it wasn't enough to give her a sense of worth. She became very depressed.

A Friend Who Lied to Her

She made a friend that would help her through these times. This friend took advantage of her and lied to her. He made her believe that he was the only thing that mattered. He made her believe that her life was worthless without him. He told her that I was a bad son and told her to cut me out of her life. He told her to cut her only sister out of her life and the majority of her friends. He told her to lie to her husband in order to continue their relationship. He made her desperate for him.

This so-called friend was alcohol.

Twenty Days Comatose

On Thanksgiving night, my mother ate her final meal and drank vodka at a constant pace until December 4 when the people who loved her most found her to be in a grave state and called 911.

She spent 20 days in the hospital. She spent most of those days comatose. When she was awake she would ask people to bring her just a little vodka to take the edge off. I saw her on December 15 which was her 60th birthday. Instead of cake and presents she got a feeding tube from the doctor and some flowers from a son who she wasn't speaking to . . . because he asked her to stop drinking.

Instead of running to the store to buy her a last minute gift, on December 23, my father, my sister and I were faced with the decision to give her death with some morphine to help ease the pain. We were not offered anything for our pain. Instead, while visions of sugar plums danced in many heads around the world, we juggled

> **FAST FACT**
>
> In 2005 a total of 21,634 persons died of alcohol-induced causes in the United States, according to the National Center for Health Statistics.

broken hearts, planned services, and tried to stay strong for our children.

Alcoholism Can Destroy a Family

My mother was an amazing person at one time. She taught me that anything worth doing is worth doing to the best of your ability. She taught me how to play cribbage and she taught me how to make a great spaghetti sauce.

She also taught me how alcoholism can destroy a family.

Addiction Will Lie to Them

My mom is survived by her husband of 33 years, a son, a daughter, three step-daughters, and eight grandchildren that have a 40 percent chance of becoming alcoholics as well.

If you have someone that you love in your life that is struggling with some kind of addiction or depression, urge them to get help before it's too late. In the long run, they can only help themselves, but if we don't show them where their life is heading, their addictions will lie to them and tell them they are fine.

One of my mother's final words were: "I am not an alcoholic."

An Alcoholic's Life Is Forever Changed

Tatiana Morales and Brian Dakss

The following story is about Joan Lovett, a former TV news anchor-woman in Chicago, and her battle with alcoholism. Joan thought she left her troubled childhood behind her when she achieved personal and professional success as a young woman. However, when her past intruded on her life, it was more than Joan could handle, and she turned to alcohol for help. When a tragedy occurred while Joan was in jail for drunk driving, she vowed to turn her life around. Tatiana Morales and Brian Dakss write for CBS News online.

Joan Lovett was great at what she did. Her work won awards. An article in a 1991 edition of *Mademoiselle* magazine pegged Joan as a rising star. But that star had a dark side. Almost from the moment she was born, Joan's life was an uphill fight.

"We lived with an alcoholic father. Our lives were generally very chaotic. Money problems. A lot of utilities

SOURCE: Tatiana Morales and Brian Dakss, "Abuse+Alcohol+Jail=A New Life, and Rising from Rock Bottom," CBS News, October 12, 13, 2004. Reproduced by permission.

turned off. Evictions. Food stamps, that sort of thing. A lot of abuse. My father was sexually abusive to me, physically abusive to my brothers. My mom had to hold down two jobs to try and keep us together."

But Joan's troubles seemed to end when she left for college, and after graduation, she got a series of jobs which eventually led her to the anchor desk at *CBS* in the Windy City [Chicago].

Feelings of Guilt

Her personal life seemed to be a success, too. She met a coworker who turned out to be her soul mate. In 1987, Joan Lovett became Mrs. Jeff Abrams. She had two kids. Her past kept intruding on her life. Joan's father, who she says had abused her as a child, became increasingly ill and became dependent on her. Joan found herself caught in an emotional minefield, between pity and rage.

He told her over the phone he was moving into a nursing home and needed a substantial amount of money to get in there. She became overwhelmed with emotion and said, "I remember everything you did. I feel like you used me. I'm tired of giving you anything. I want you out of my life."

Not long after she spoke those words, Joan's father died. That angry outburst would be the last thing she ever said to him and her feelings of guilt began to tear her apart.

"I turned to drinking. And I kept my job. I did my job," she says.

Her performance veered from a wreck to top notch.

"I won my Emmys, I was functional but I knew I had to have a drink to make the pain go away," she says.

In the late 1990s, there was a big shake-up at the station and, eventually, Joan was let go. She looked for a job and Jeff looked for a job. Eventually, he found something in Baltimore, and the whole family relocated. But that change of scenery didn't do Joan any good. In fact, it made things worse.

"I thought that I would stay home and help the kids with the transition, and started drinking more and more. I drank in the morning. I drank while they were at school. Terrible things happened. Some days, they would come home, I would be passed out."

Jail and Tragedy

Joan's addiction to alcohol led to a series of drunk-driving arrests and that last offense in August 2002 landed her in jail.

"I thought that life could never be worse than that. It was hideously, incomprehensibly demoralizing," she says.

With Joan locked up, Jeff took on the job of raising the two kids alone.

Many alcoholics must hit bottom before they are able to turn their lives around.
(© Shawshots/Alamy)

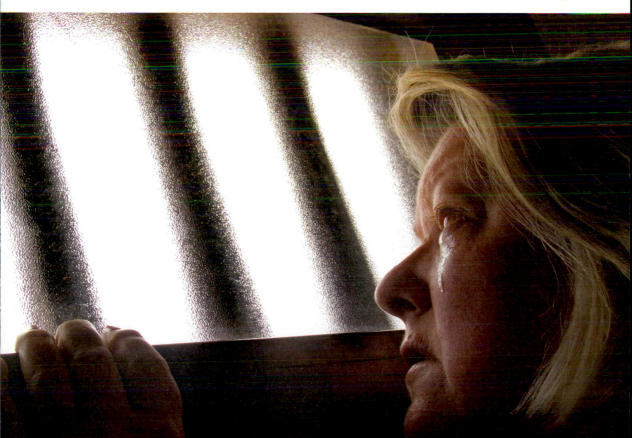

"Jeff would have to make dinner. Jeff had to take them to practices. Jeff took over."

Somehow, Jeff managed to hold the family together, until the morning of Oct. 10, 2002.

His routine was to go for a jog at 5 a.m., come home, cool down, and get the kids up for school.

One morning, Jeff collapsed on his morning run, just a few feet from his house.

"My daughter called a neighbor and said, 'Daddy didn't come home from his jog.' And the neighbor came over and at that point, a police officer finally showed up and said, 'Your daddy is dead.'"

Twenty-three miles away inside the county detention center, prison officials told Joan Lovett that she was a widow. She asked to attend the funeral but her request was denied.

"When I got that news in jail, I collapsed onto the floor and then I got on to my knees and I prayed for my kids and then I said, 'God, please help me find a way to live.'"

Before long, her prayer would be answered. . . .

Getting Her Life Back Together

"Sometimes I think back on those terrible things but I know I was a sick person," Joan reflected.

"While she was behind bars, Joan's two kids were staying with her brother and his wife in Missouri. And when she was released in April of 2003, Joan went to St. Louis to reclaim her family, and try to put her life back together.

"I was in control at that point," she says.

Now, with the help of a 12-step program, Joan has turned everything around. "I don't dwell on the past. For me, I guess coming to the brink of death, and losing everything, and now having what I have, it's a miracle. It's a thrill."

In her darkest days, before going to jail, Joan tried to take her own life. She severed tendons in the process, and is now trying to re-learn the piano.

Joan completed substance-abuse counseling, but knows there are no guarantees—and that her family will be together only as long as she stays sober: "I've been sober long enough to know that the 12-step program I'm in works. My belief in a higher power works. And this is a better way of life."

Joan says she takes life one day at a time, and admits she can't promise she won't take a drink tomorrow.

Now, Joan has become the mom she always wanted to be.

Thanks to some wise investments, she doesn't have to go back to work right away. She's available to her kids, and to other women with substance-abuse problems.

Sammy and Jonathan are both straight-A students, and Joan's life revolves around them rather than finding her next drink. "It's a miracle to me that they want me in their lives like that, after everything they've been through," she marvels.

> **FAST FACT**
>
> According to Mothers Against Drunk Driving, over 1.46 million American drivers were arrested in 2006 for driving under the influence of alcohol or narcotics.

Forgiveness

Joan got her family back, but something else was tormenting her. Her husband, Jeff, died while she was locked up, and she never had the chance to say goodbye.

"I couldn't do anything if Jeff was gonna enter my mind, because I would break down," she says. "One night earlier this year, I prayed to God, I said, 'I'm not angry anymore. I just want to forgive myself, so that I can go on.'"

Joan traveled to Chicago and visited Jeff's grave for the first time—to ask forgiveness from the man she felt she had failed in life. The next morning, she went back one more time—to say goodbye.

"I would have died a long time ago if Jeff hadn't been there. And he'll always be my love. And [I] also know Jeff wants me to move on," Joan says.

[A friend] asked Joan, "If he could see . . . you now, because in the end he had an awful picture of what had become of you, what would he think?

"I think," Joan answered, "he would say, 'I told you that you could do it.'"

GLOSSARY

acetaldehyde   One of the first products of the body's metabolism of alcohol. Acetaldehyde is then converted to carbon dioxide and water, which are excreted from the body.

acute   Of abrupt onset, in reference to a disease. Acute often also connotes an illness that is of short duration, rapidly progressive, and in need of urgent care.

addiction   A state that involves a physical or psychological dependency on a drug or alcohol.

Al-anon and Alateen   A fellowship of relatives, particularly spouses and children, and friends of alcoholics who share their experiences, strength, and hope in order to solve their common problems.

alcohol abuse   The continued use of alcohol despite the development of social, legal, or health problems.

alcohol dehydrogenase (ADH)   An enzyme found in the liver and stomach that helps break down alcohol into substances that can be excreted from the body. Specifically, ADH converts alcohol into acetaldehyde, which is then converted into carbon dioxide and water.

alcoholic hepatitis   Inflammation of the liver caused by chronic ingestion of alcohol.

alcoholic liver diseases   Diseases caused by excessive drinking, which include fatty liver, or steatosis; liver inflammation, or hepatitis; and cirrhosis.

Alcoholics Anonymous (AA)   A worldwide fellowship of men and women who share a desire to stop drinking alcohol. AA suggests members completely abstain from alcohol, regularly attend meetings with other members, and follow its program to help each other. AA is the original 12-step program.

alcoholism   A chronic disease (sometimes also called alcohol addiction or alcohol dependence) characterized by a strong craving for alcohol, a constant or periodic reliance on the use of alcohol despite adverse consequences, the inability to limit drinking, physical illness when drinking is stopped, and the need for increasing amounts of alcohol to feel its effects.

Antabuse   The brand name for disulfiram, the first drug approved to treat alcohol dependence. Antabuse produces an acute sensitivity to alcohol, which causes a highly unpleasant reaction when the patient ingests even small amounts of alcohol.

binge drinking   Drinking five or more drinks in a row on a single occasion for a man or four or more drinks for a woman.

blood alcohol concentration (BAC)   The amount of alcohol in the blood expressed as a percent: grams of ethanol per 100 milliliters (deciliter) of blood.

CAGE questionnaire   A diagnostic tool used to assess individuals for potential alcohol problems, including dependence.

cirrhosis   A consequence of chronic liver disease characterized by replacement of liver tissue by fibrous scar tissue as well as regenerative nodules, leading to progressive loss of liver function. Cirrhosis is most commonly caused by alcoholism, hepatitis B and C, and fatty liver disease.

delirium tremens (DTs)   A serious alcohol-withdrawal syndrome observed in persons who stop drinking alcohol following continuous and heavy consumption. It involves profound confusion, hallucinations, and severe nervous system overactivity, typically beginning between forty-eight and ninety-six hours after the last drink.

depressant   A substance that causes sedation and drowsiness. Alcohol is a central nervous system depressant.

detoxification   An abrupt stop of alcohol drinking coupled with the substitution of drugs that have similar effects to prevent alcohol withdrawal.

Diagnostic and Statistical Manual of Mental Disorders, 4th edition (*DSM-IV*)	A book published by the American Psychiatric Association that gives general descriptions and characteristic symptoms of different mental illnesses. Physicians and other mental health professionals use the *DSM-IV* to confirm diagnoses for mental illnesses. The next edition of the *DSM* is scheduled for 2011.
dipsomania	A historical term used in the nineteenth century to describe a medical condition involving an uncontrollable craving for alcohol.
dopamine	A neurotransmitter that is affected by alcohol and regulates brain processes such as those that control movements, emotions, pleasure, and pain.
fibrosis	An accumulation of tough, fibrous scar tissue in the liver.
functional tolerance	A state in which a chronic alcohol abuser learns to function under the influence of alcohol. The impairment normally associated with performing a familiar task is reduced, but the ability to perform unfamiliar tasks remains impaired.
GABA	Gamma-aminobutyric acid, a neurotransmitter affected by alcohol.
gastritis	An inflammation of the stomach lining.
glutamate	A neurotransmitter that regulates brain processes such as learning and memory and that is affected by alcohol.
hepatic	Having to do with the liver. From the Latin *hepaticus*, derived from the Greek *hepar*, meaning "the liver."
hepatic encephalopathy	Brain dysfunction directly due to liver dysfunction, most often recognized in advanced liver disease. Hepatic encephalopathy may cause disturbances of consciousness and progress to coma.
hepatitis	Inflammation of the liver from any cause.
hepatitis C	Inflammation of the liver due to the hepatitis C virus (HCV), which is usually spread by blood transfusion, hemodialysis, and needle sticks. HCV can lead to cirrhosis and cancer. Hepatitis C is common in alcoholics, and alcohol worsens the symptoms of hepatitis C. Previously known as non-A, non-B hepatitis.

impairment	Diminished ability, such as when alcohol decreases motor function or interferes with thinking.
inebriety	A term used between 1870 and 1920 to describe habitual drunkenness.
jaundice	Yellow staining of the skin and sclerae (the whites of the eyes) by abnormally high blood levels of the bile pigment bilirubin caused by liver diseases.
neurotransmitters	Chemical substances that transmit information between neurons.
relapse	To fall back or revert to an earlier state; to regress after partial recovery. In the context of alcohol abuse and alcoholism, relapse means to start drinking again after giving up alcohol.
reward pathway	A specialized network of neurons in the brain that produce and regulate pleasure associated with eating, drinking, and sex. These neurons use dopamine as a neurotransmitter. Alcohol activates the reward pathway.
sobriety	The condition of refraining from drinking alcohol.
steatosis	An accumulation of fat in liver cells, also known as fatty liver. Commonly seen in alcoholics.
tolerance	The body's ability to adapt to chronic alcohol or substance use.
12-step program	A program based on a set of guiding principles outlining a course of action for recovery from addiction, compulsion, or other behavioral problems.
Wernicke-Korsakoff syndrome	A brain disease caused by a severe shortage of thiamine (vitamin B1), which is commonly caused by continuous, excessive alcohol intake.
withdrawal	Severe alcohol cravings as well as physical and psychological problems caused by the withdrawal from excessive, chronic alcohol consumption. The biochemical changes lead to short-term memory loss, disruption of cognitive and motor function, reduced perceptual abilities, and emotional and personality changes that include acts of aggression.

CHRONOLOGY

B.C.

ca. 10,000 Discovery of late Stone Age beer jugs has established the fact that intentionally fermented beverages existed at least as early as the Neolithic period.

ca. 4000 Wine appears as a finished product in Egyptian pictographs.

ca. 460–370 Hippocrates identifies numerous medicinal properties of wine.

ca. 429–351 Xenophon and Plato praise the moderate use of wine as beneficial to health and happiness and are critical of drunkenness.

A.D

ca. 1350–1400 Consumption of distilled beverages rises dramatically in Europe, as distilled liquors are commonly used as remedies for the Black Death.

ca. 1500 Swiss physician, alchemist, and philosopher Paracelsus is the first person to use the term *alcohol* (from the Arabic word that means "finely divided").

ca. 1500–1600 Drinking alcohol is a way of life in Britain, partly to avoid drinking contaminated water.

ca. 1600–1700 American colonists regard alcohol as the "good creature of God."

1761 Italian Giovanni Battista Morgagni, known as the father of modern anatomical pathology, identifies a peculiar transformation of the liver, which will later be called cirrhosis.

1784 American physician Benjamin Rush, a signer of the Declaration of Independence, writes "An Enquiry into the Effects of Spirituous Liquors upon the Human Body, and Their Influence upon the Happiness of Society," in which he develops the concept of habitual drinking as a form of medical disease.

1804 Scottish physician Thomas Trotter writes "An Essay, Medical, Philosophical and Chemical on Drunkenness and its Effects on the Human Body," in which he characterizes excessive drinking as a disease or medical condition.

1819 Dipsomania, a historical term describing a medical condition involving an uncontrollable craving for alcohol, is first coined by the German physician C.W. Hufeland.

1819 French physician René Laënnec, inventor of the stethoscope, gives cirrhosis its name, using the Greek word for "tawny," *kirrhos*, referring to the tawny, yellow nodules characteristic of the disease.

1826 The American Society for the Promotion of Temperance is founded.

1849 Magnus Huss writes "Alcoholismus Chronicus, or Chronic Alcohol Illness. A Contribution to the Study of Dyscrasias Based on My Personal Experience and the Experience of Others" and introduces the term *alcoholism* for the first time.

1870 The American Association for the Cure of Inebriates forms and declares that intemperance is "an illness caused by an inherited or acquired constitutional susceptibility to alcohol and can be cured as other diseases are."

1876 A section of the American Medical Association declares that inebriates require special institutions.

1880 Leslie Keeley announces he has found a cure for alcoholism and addiction; he calls it "bichloride of gold."

1893 The Massachusetts Hospital for Dipsomaniacs and Inebriates opens.

1910 The first "driving under the influence" (DUI) laws are enacted in New York State.

1920 Prohibition begins with the passage of the Eighteenth Amendment to the U.S. Constitution, which prohibits the manufacture, transportation, and sale of intoxicating beverages.

1930 The first theory as to the pathogenesis of liver cirrhosis is advanced by German pathologist Robert Rossle.

1933 The Twenty-first Amendment to the U.S. Constitution repeals the Eighteenth Amendment, and Prohibition ends.

1935 Stockbroker Bill Wilson and physician Robert Smith form Alcoholics Anonymous (AA) with the belief that an alcoholic is unable to control his or her drinking and recovery is possible only with total abstinence and peer support.

1950s   Doctors are aware of various alcohol problems as well as the relationship between alcoholism and diseases such as the degeneration of the liver, gastritis, and hepatic cirrhosis.

1951   The World Health Organization (WHO) calls alcoholism a serious medical problem.

1951   The U.S. Food and Drug Administration approves disulfiram, also known as Antabuse, for the treatment of alcoholism.

1956   The American Medical Association declares alcoholism a treatable illness.

1960   Physician Elvin Jellinek publishes his book *The Disease Concept of Alcoholism*, which forms the basis for the modern theory of alcoholism as a disease.

1965   The American Psychiatric Association begins to use the term *disease* to describe alcoholism.

1968   The second edition of the *Diagnostic and Statistical Manual of Mental Disorders* (*DSM-II*) includes alcoholism in the section dealing with personality disorders and certain other nonpsychotic mental disorders. The *DSM-II* divides alcoholism into three subcategories: episodic excessive drinking, habitual excessive drinking, and alcohol addiction.

1973   David Smith, Ken Jones, and others coin the term *fetal alcohol syndrome* to describe a pattern of birth defects found in children of mothers who consumed alcohol during pregnancy.

1980   The third edition of the *Diagnostic and Statistical Manual of Mental Disorders* (*DSM-III*) drops the term *alcoholism* in favor of two distinct categories labeled "alcohol abuse" and "alcohol dependence." Additionally, the *DSM-III* categorizes alcohol abuse and dependence as substance use disorders, rather than as subsets of personality disorders.

1980   Mothers Against Drunk Driving (MADD) forms.

1989   Social psychologist Stanton Peele publishes his book *The Diseasing of America*, in which he argues that AA and for-profit alcohol treatment centers promote the "myth" of alcoholism as a lifelong disease.

1992   The Joint Committee of the National Council on Alcoholism and Drug Dependence and the American Society of Addiction Medicine publish a definition of alcoholism in *The Journal of the American Medical Association* (*JAMA*), which says that "alcoholism is a primary chronic disease with genetic, psychosocial, and environmental factors influencing its development and manifestations. The disease is often progressive and fatal. It is characterized by impaired control over drinking, preoccupation with the drug alcohol, use of alcohol despite adverse consequences, and distortions in thinking, mostly denial. Each of these symptoms may be continuous or periodic."

2004   The World Health Organization estimates that there are about 2 billion people worldwide who consume alcoholic beverages and 76.3 million with diagnosable alcohol-use disorders.

ORGANIZATIONS TO CONTACT

The editors have compiled the following list of organizations concerned with the issues debated in this book. The descriptions are derived from materials provided by the organizations. All have publications or information available for interested readers. The list was compiled on the date of publication of the present volume; the information provided here may change. Be aware that many organizations take several weeks or longer to respond to inquiries, so allow as much time as possible.

Al-anon and Alateen
1600 Corporate
Landing Pkwy.
Virginia Beach, VA
23454-5617
(757) 563-1600
fax: (757) 563-1655
e-mail: wso@al-anon
.org
www.al-anon.alateen
.org

Al-anon and Alateen are fellowship groups for the spouses, children, and other relatives and friends of alcoholics. Al-anon and Alateen are 12-step programs that provide comfort, understanding and encouragement to the relatives of the alcoholic and to the alcoholics themselves. Al-anon and Alateen publishes *The Forum*, a monthly magazine.

Alcoholics Anonymous (AA)
A.A. World Services,
Inc.
PO Box 459
New York, NY 10163
(212) 870-3400
www.aa.org

AA is a voluntary, worldwide fellowship of men and women who gather together to attain and maintain sobriety. AA espouses a 12-step program to help people with alcohol disorders stay sober. The AA Web site provides various AA literature as well as access to AA's international magazine, *AA Grapevine*—known as a "meeting in print."

American Council on Alcoholism (ACA)
1000 E. Indian
School Rd.
Phoenix, AZ 85014
(800) 527-5344
fax: (602) 264-7403
e-mail: info@aca-usa
.org
www.aca-usa.org

The ACA is an information and referral service for individuals who suffer from alcohol dependence, their families, treatment professionals, and the general public who are seeking a broad range of information on alcohol, alcohol dependence, alcohol abuse, and options for recovery.

American Society of Addiction Medicine (ASAM)
4601 N. Park Ave.
Upper Arcade
Ste.101
Chevy Chase, MD
20815
(301) 656-3920
fax: (301) 656-3815
email @asam.org
www.asam.org

The ASAM is composed of physicians and researchers who are interested in addiction medicine. The society seeks to improve the care and treatment of people who suffer from addictions and to advance the practice of addiction medicine. The *Journal of Addiction Medicine* is the official journal of the ASAM. The organization's newsletter is called the *ASAM News*.

International Society for Biomedical Research on Alcoholism (ISBRA)
PO Box 202332
Denver, CO
80220-8332
(303) 355-6420
fax: (303) 355-1207
e-mail: isbra@isbra
.com
www.isbra.com

ISBRA's mission is to promote excellence internationally in all aspects of biomedical research on alcoholism and alcohol-related biomedical phenomena. *Alcoholism: Clinical and Experimental Research*, which brings readers the latest clinical studies and research findings on alcoholism and alcohol-induced syndromes, is the official journal of ISBRA and the Research Society on Alcoholism.

National Association for Children of Alcoholics (NACoA)
11426 Rockville Pike
Ste. 301
Rockville, MD 20852
(888) 554-2627 or
(301) 468-0985
fax: (301) 468-0987
e-mail: nacoa@nacoa
.org
www.nacoa.org

The NACoA is a national nonprofit organization working on behalf of children of alcohol and drug dependent parents. The organization works to raise public awareness; provide leadership in public policy at the national, state, and local levels; advocate for appropriate, effective, and accessible education and prevention services; and facilitate and advance professional knowledge and understanding. The NACoA publishes a newsletter, *The Network*, and several guides for parents and teens.

National Center on Addiction and Substance Abuse at Columbia University (CASA)
633 Third Ave.
19th Fl.
New York, NY
10017-6706
(212) 841-5200
www.casacolumbia
.org

CASA is a private, nonprofit organization that works to educate the public about the costs and hazards of substance abuse and the prevention and treatment of all forms of chemical dependency. CASA supports treatment as the best way to reduce drug and alcohol addiction. The organization publishes many books and reports assessing the state of substance abuse in America. Additionally, the center's newsletter, *CASAINSIDE*, is published three times each year.

National Clearinghouse for Alcohol and Drug Information (NCADI)
PO Box 2345
Rockville, MD
20847-2345
(800) 729-6686
e-mail: https://
ncadistore.samhsa
.gov/email/
http://ncadi.samhsa
.gov/

The NCADI distributes publications of the U.S. Department of Health and Human Services, the National Institute on Drug Abuse, and other federal agencies concerned with alcohol and drug abuse. Brochure titles include *Tips for Teens: The Truth About Alcohol* and *Underage Drinking: Myths vs. Facts.*

National Council on Alcoholism and Drug Dependence (NCADD)
244 E. Fifty-eighth St.
4th Fl.
New York, NY 10022
(212) 269-7797
fax: (212) 269-7510
e-mail: national@
ncadd.org
www.ncadd.org

The NCADD provides education, information, help, and hope to the public. The council advocates prevention, intervention, and treatment through a nationwide network of affiliates. In addition, NCADD operates a toll-free Hope Line (800-622-2255) for information and referral and a National Intervention Network (800-654-4673) to educate and assist the families and friends of addicted persons. The NCADD Web site offers various booklets, fact sheets, and brochures about alcoholism treatment and prevention.

National Institute for Alcohol Abuse and Alcoholism (NIAAA)
5635 Fishers Ln.
MSC 9304
Bethesda, MD
20892-9304
(301) 443-3860
e-mail: niaaaweb-r@
exchange.nih.gov
www.niaaa.nih.gov

The NIAAA, a branch of the National Institutes of Health, is the U.S. agency charged with reducing alcohol-related problems through supporting research, disseminating findings, and collaborating with other institutions, nationally and internationally. NIAAA publications include *Alcohol Alert* and *Alcohol Research and Health.*

Substance Abuse and Mental Health Services Administration (SAMHSA)
Center for Mental Health Services
1 Choke Cherry Rd.
Rockville, MD 20857
(240) 276-1310
fax: (240) 276-1320
e-mail:
shin@samhsa.hhs
.gov
www.samhsa.gov

SAMHSA, part of the U.S. Department of Health and Human Services, seeks to ensure that people who suffer from mental health or substance abuse disorders have the opportunity to live fulfilling and meaningful lives. SAMHSA works to expand and enhance prevention and early intervention programs and improve the quality, availability, and range of mental health and substance abuse treatment and support services in local communities across the United States. The agency publishes a bimonthly newsletter, *SAMSHA News,* as well as various recurring statistical reports on mental health and substance abuse.

FOR FURTHER READING

Books

Susan Cheever, *My Name Is Bill: Bill Wilson; His Life and Creation of Alcoholics Anonymous.* New York: Simon & Schuster, 2004.

Columbia University, National Center on Addiction and Substance Abuse, *Women Under the Influence.* Baltimore: Johns Hopkins University Press, 2006.

Carlton Erickson, *The Science of Addiction: From Neurobiology to Treatment.* New York: Norton, 2007.

Janet Lynne Golden, *Message in a Bottle: The Making of Fetal Alcohol Syndrome.* Cambridge, MA: Harvard University Press, 2005.

The Healing Project, Charles Beem, and Joseph Califano, *Voices of Alcoholism: The Healing Companion; Stories for Courage, Comfort, and Strength.* Brooklyn, NY: LaChance, 2008.

Jack E. Henningfield, Patrica B. Santora, and Warren K. Bickel, *Addiction Treatment: Science and Policy for the Twenty-first Century.* Baltimore: Johns Hopkins University Press, 2007.

Jeff Herten, *An Uncommon Drunk: Revelations of a High-Functioning Alcoholic.* Bloomington, IN: iUniverse, 2006.

John Hoffman and Susan Froemke, *Addiction: Why Can't They Just Stop? New Knowledge, New Treatments, New Hope.* New York: Rodale, 2007.

William Cope Moyers and Katherine Ketcham, *Broken: My Story of Addiction and Redemption.* New York: Viking, 2006.

David Sheff, *Beautiful Boy: A Father's Journey Through His Son's Addiction.* Boston: Houghton Mifflin, 2008.

Doug Thorburn, *Alcoholism Myths and Realities: Removing the Stigma of Society's Most Destructive Disease.* Northridge, CA: Galt, 2005.

Sarah Tracy, *Alcoholism in America: From Reconstruction to Prohibition.* Baltimore: Johns Hopkins University Press, 2005.

Periodicals

Buffalo (NY) News, "Just Say No: Pregnant Women Should Avoid Alcohol for Baby's Sake," April 3, 2007.

Charles Bush, "Doctor Keeley's Gold Cure," *History Magazine,* February/March 2009.

Eva Carner, "Eva & Rick's Incredible Journey," *Exceptional Parent,* November 2006.

Cincinnati Post, "Brain Atrophy Linked to Alcoholism," January 16, 2007.

Robert Davis, "Alcohol-Saturated 'Fun' Can Be Lethal," *USA Today,* August 22, 2007.

Norman Giesbrecht, "Is Alcohol a Risk Factor for Trauma and Chronic Disease Mortality? Narrowing the Gap Between Evidence and Action," *American Journal of Epidemiology,* 2008.

Jessica Griggs, "Babies Are OK After Light Drinking in Pregnancy," *New Scientist,* October 2008.

Harvard Health Publications, "Excess Drinking May Lead to Depression," *Harvard Reviews of Health News,* March 4, 2009.

Ivan Hewett, "High Notes from the Horn of Africa: Through Alcoholism and Apartheid, Hugh Masekela Has Always Made Music That Is Resolutely Cheerful," *Daily Telegraph* (UK), April 25, 2009.

Joseph W. LaBrie et al. "What Men Want: The Role of Reflective Opposite-Sex Normative Preferences in Alcohol Use Among College Women," *Psychology of Addictive Behaviors,* 2009.

Patricia McDaniel and Ruth Malone, "The Role of Corporate Credibility in Legitimizing Disease Promotion," *American Journal of Public Health*, March 2009.

National Institute on Alcohol Abuse and Alcoholism, "Alcoholic Liver Disease, Part I: An Overview," *Alcohol Research and Health*, 2003.

Chantel Sloan, Vicki Sayarath, and Jason Moore, "Systems Genetics of Alcoholism," *Alcohol Research & Health*, 2008.

Dimitri Vassilaros, "Hope for Anybody," *Pittsburgh Tribune-Review*, December 26, 2008.

Women's Health Weekly, "Is It Really About Alcohol? The Truth About Alcohol Abuse in Women," April 9, 2009.

Internet Sources

David J. Hanson, Alcohol Problems and Solutions. www2.pots dam.edu/hansondj.

Medical News Today, "Coffee Protects Alcohol Drinkers from Liver Disease," June 13, 2006. www.medicalnewstoday.com/ articles/ 45124.php.

————, "Drinking Alcohol and Benefits," July 20, 2003. www.medicalnewstoday.com/articles/3968.php.

Catharine Munro, "Younger Brains 'Tricked' by Alcohol," *Age*, April 29, 2009. www.theage.com.au/lifestyle/wellbeing/younger-brains-tricked-by-alcohol-20090428-amlh.html.

Rutgers University, Center of Alcohol Studies. http://alcohol studies.rutgers.edu/index.html.

ScienceDaily, "Liver Disease Responsible for Most Alcohol-Related Illness and Deaths." April 24, 2009. www.sciencedaily .com/releases/2009/04/090423082640.htm.

INDEX

Smithers, R. Brinkley, 77, 78
Sobell, Linda, 126–127
Sobell, Mark, 126–127
Sokol, Robert, 12
Solomon, Melanie, 119
The Stages of Alcoholism (Jellinek), 78
Substance-abuse treatment, *70*
Suicidal thought, 95–96
Surveys
  on alcoholism as disease, 79
  on student substance abuse, 92–94, 102
Sustachek, Jon, 129, 133–134, 135–136

T
Temperance movement, 77
Thiamine, deficiency of, 24, 47
Tobacco dependence, genetic profile for, 34
Treatment, 22–24
  alternative, 25–26
  believing it is not needed, *126*
  as industry, 78, 79
  number of people needing, *70*, 72
  programs that teach choice 86
  variation by subtype 43–44
  See also Medications
12-step programs, 24, 49, 80
  are effective, 107–118
  are helpful to some alcoholics, 71–72
  are not effective, 119–127
  are resistant to use of medication, 70–71
  steps in, 112–116
  success of, 31

U
United States
  deaths from alcohol abuse in, 66, 145
  obesity in, 104
  percent of adults drinking alcohol, *81*

V
Vacovsky, Lloyd, 123
Vivitrex, 47, 50

W
Weber, Sue, 137
Wechsler, Henry, 100
Wells, Ken R., 15
Wernicke's syndrome, 19, 23, 24, 47
White, Aaron M., 97
Wisconsin, 131–133, 134–135
Withdrawal symptoms, 23
World Health Organization (WHO), 52

Y
Yoast, Richard, 133
Young adults
  binge drinking and, *98*
  prevalence of alcohol dependence, 42